A SCHOOL-AGE CARE PROGRAM GUIDE

Child Development Division
California Department of Education

Publishing Information

Kids' Time: A School-Age Care Program Guide was developed by the Child Development Division, California Department of Education, working in cooperation with the School-Age Care Work Group. See Acknowledgments on pages vii and viii for the names of those who participated in the development and review of the document. The principal writer was Betsy Arns.

This publication was edited by Sheila Bruton, working in cooperation with Barbara Tardif, Child Development Consultant, California Department of Education. It was designed and prepared for photo-offset production by the staff of the Bureau of Publications, with the cover and interior design created and prepared by Steve Yee. Typesetting was done by Carey Johnson. Photography was by Glen Korengold.

It was published by the Department of Education, 721 Capitol Mall, Sacramento, California (mailing address: P.O. Box 944272, Sacramento, CA 94244-2720). It was printed by the Office of State Printing and distributed under the provisions of the Library Distribution Act and *Government Code* Section 11096.

ISBN 0-8011-1155-2

Ordering Information

Copies of this publication are available for $10.50 each, plus sales tax for California residents, from the Bureau of Publications, Sales Unit, California Department of Education, P.O. Box 271, Sacramento, CA 95812-0271; FAX (916) 323-0823. See page 156 for complete information on payment, including credit card purchases.

A partial list of other educational resources available from the Department appears on pages 155-56. In addition, a 68-page illustrated *Publications Catalog* and supplement describing the content of educational resources available from the Department can be obtained without charge by writing to the address given above or by calling the Sales Unit at (916) 445-1260.

Notice

The guidance in *Kids' Time: A School-Age Care Program Guide* is not binding on local educational agencies or other entities. Except for the statutes, regulations, and court decisions that are referenced herein, the guide is exemplary, and compliance with it is not mandatory. (See *Education Code* Section 33308.5.)

Contents

List of Tables

Preface

The Child Development Division of the California Department of Education provides funds for many different kinds of child care and development programs, and one of the division's primary goals is the consistent growth and improvement of those programs. Therefore, the division develops materials to assist agencies in program development, enhancement, and self-evaluation.

This document is the first program guide developed specifically for all school-age care programs. It is designed and intended to accompany the publication *Exemplary Program Standards for Child Development Programs Serving Preschool and School-Age Children* and to expand on the concepts addressed in that document. The intent of that document was to set standards for programs that serve children from three to fourteen years of age in a variety of settings, including center-based programs, such as school-age care, and family child care programs. The purpose of this program guide is to specify what an exemplary school-age care (SAC) program for children five to fourteen years old would look like and to help the staff develop such a program or improve its existing program.

This guide was developed by the California Department of Education for use by all SAC programs. The Department provides funding for school-age care programs that serve low-income families in which the parents have particular needs, work, go to school, or are in training and need school-age care to meet those obligations. Other fee-paying families are also included in school-age care. In addition, the Department provides small start-up SAC grants for groups and organizations wishing to start their own before- and after-school programs. The Department's purpose in funding various kinds of SAC programs is to promote the formation of high-quality SAC programs for families throughout California. The Department intends to continue taking a leadership position in expanding this kind of exemplary care.

ROBERT W. AGEE
Deputy Superintendent
Field Services Branch

ROBERT A. CERVANTES
Assistant Superintendent
Child Development Division

KATHRYN L. WITCHER
Manager
Program Development and Improvement Unit
Child Development Division

Acknowledgments

Many people contributed to the preparation of this document. The following persons, representing a wide variety of programs, were members of the School-Age Care (SAC) Work Group that helped develop the content of the guide:

Principal Writer: **Betsy Arns,** Author; Lecturer, Counselor/Teacher, Costa Mesa High School, Newport-Mesa Unified School District

Work Group Chair: **Sandy Litzie,** Supervisor, Child Care Coordination, City of Irvine

Work Group Members: **Sue Bohlen,** Program Director, Fountain Valley Elementary School District Extended Day Care Program; **Mary Hampton,** Program Director, Child Development, Garvey Elementary School District; **Rick Porter,** Executive Director, Rainbow River and Rainbow Rising School-Age Care Programs; **Jan Shively,** Program Director, Claremont Unified School District Extended Day Care Program; **Melinda Sprague,** Private Consultant, School-Age Care Programs; **Alison Stewart,** Children/Teen Supervisor, Recreation Center for the Handicapped; and **Don Williams,** Program Development Specialist, Riverside County Office of Education

Resource Persons: **Shirley Adams,** Program Development Specialist, Riverside County Office of Education; **Suzanne Porter,** Anti-Bias Curriculum Consultant, Rainbow River and Rainbow Rising School-Age Care Programs; and **Annette Unten,** Instructor, Orange Coast College

California Department of Education Staff Representative: **Barbara Tardif,** Child Development Consultant

Special acknowledgment is given to Betsy Arns, who served as the principal writer of this guide. With her creative ability and writing skill, she was able to blend the ideas of the work group with her own wide SAC knowledge and experience. Additional recognition goes to Sandy Litzie, chair of the work group, who always kept the group on task and lent to it her special organizational skills, and to Barbara Tardif, who provided guidance to the committee and also wrote portions of the document.

Several other California Department of Education staff members provided special time, consideration, and effort in finalizing this document. Particular thanks is given to **Kathryn Witcher,** Manager, Program Development and Improvement Unit, Child Development Division, for her ongoing leadership, experience, and support; **Robert Cervantes,** Assistant Superintendent, Child Development Division, for his ideas and analytical skills; and **Robert Agee,** Deputy Superintendent, Field Services Branch, for his vision of what a quality California Department of Education school-age care publication would be like.

Additional contributions were made by staff members in other units of the Department, including the Curriculum Frameworks and Instructional Resources Office and the Elementary Education Office, Curriculum and Instructional Leadership Branch. Thanks are also due to **Joan Hanssmann,** student intern, for contributing her child development expertise and editing skills.

Lastly, special thanks are due to **Karen Valech,** Child Care Program Supervisor, City of Sacramento 4th R Program, for allowing photographs to be taken of children in the school-age care program.

Philosophy for School-Age Care Programs

This document is based on the principle that school-age care programs exist for the purpose of promoting, nurturing, supporting, and enhancing all areas of children's development. Basic to the purpose is the assumption that all children are individuals of equal worth and value who come to the program at their own developmental level and bring with them a unique mixture of family background, language and culture, personality, and learning style. The programs we create must serve all children and their families, and we must constantly seek ways to accommodate the unique needs of the populations served by the programs, including the needs of children with disabilities. School-age care programs must serve as a bridge between home and school. They should provide a balance of educational, social, and recreational opportunities so that the programs are special for the children in their care. They should provide an environment and activities that are conducive to all children learning in a fun, playful way. Programs should provide a safe, structured environment, one that in many ways is also informal and homelike and that responds to the children's emerging needs and interests. The programs should establish partnerships with the children's parents, elementary schools, and communities to ensure that the programs meet the needs of the whole child.

Chapter 1

Introducing School-Age Care Programs

Many people who are new to school-age care (SAC) or who have seen a limited number of SAC programs wonder what an exemplary program may be like. And people who are experienced in school-age care may want general information to share with parents and other people in the community. This chapter provides an overview of SAC programs, including descriptions of the children who are served, the places where the programs operate, staffing, and the different kinds of schedules offered.

Whom Do SAC Programs Serve?

SAC programs may be provided for children in kindergarten through grade eight. Usually, the programs serve children only in kindergarten through grade six or whatever grades are represented in the particular schools served by the program. Some programs serve only kindergarten through grade three or only middle school students (grades six, seven, and eight). The majority of the programs offered are for children in kindergarten through grade three because those children are most in need of direct supervision and care.

Most programs are open to all students who attend a specific school or schools. More and more programs are making attempts to serve children from special education programs. These children may be older than their peer group but have similar developmental levels.

Where Do SAC Programs Operate?

School-age care programs operate in a variety of settings. Many centers are located on school sites so that children do not have to be transported. Some programs are fortunate enough to have classrooms or portable buildings designated for their sole use, and others must use shared space before and after school. During the school day the shared spaces are used for other purposes, including use as cafeterias, multi-purpose rooms, libraries, or classrooms. Other programs operate in such facilities as churches, park recreation centers, public libraries, or buildings used by community agencies. Each site is unique and has its own advantages and disadvantages.

Who Are the Staff in SAC Programs?

The configuration of staff varies from program to program. All programs have some kind of site administrator, but that person may be a lead teacher who is supervised by a program coordinator or regional supervisor with responsibility for several programs; or the person may be a director who has responsibility for a particular center. Programs are administered in such a way that the needs of the children and parents can be met within a given structure.

The staff who deal directly with children are called by many titles, such as teacher, counselor, group leader, child-care provider, or aide, depending on the program structure and the person's level of responsibility. These positions are filled by many people, including people with degrees in fields such as child development, recreation, or physical education; credentialed elementary and secondary teachers; child development teachers with children's center permits; college students; parents; and community members. In programs licensed in California, teachers must have earned at least 12 semester units in appropriate course work, such as courses in early childhood education/child development, elementary education, school-age care, or recreation, that prepares them for working with the unique needs of school-age children. In high-quality programs teachers will have a combination of training and experience with school-age children that allows them to plan and carry out appropriate activities for school-age children out of school.

How Is the Day Organized?

There are four kinds of days in most SAC programs: the before-school and after-school days when school is in session; extended days when school closes early for teacher conferences or training; full days when school is closed for vacation or teacher in-service training; and full days that include before- and after-school programs and year-round school breaks. Each kind of day has a different schedule and rhythm (see Table 1 for sample schedules).

Before- and After-School Days

Most programs open early in the morning (normally between 6:30 and 7:00 a.m.). In some centers breakfast is served. The children engage in low-key activities, such as working with puzzles, games, or blocks, chosen by the individual child. Elaborate, planned projects are not usually offered in the hours before school. Some older children use the time to do homework or study for the day's tests. Most programs try to keep children from getting too wound up before they leave for school.

After school, children either walk to the program from their classrooms or use program transportation (bus or van) to reach the site. Children return at various times in the afternoon, depending on the school's release time for each grade level. Usually, kindergartners are released just before or after lunchtime; children in the primary grades are released in mid-afternoon (about 2:00 to 2:30 p.m.); and pupils in the upper grades are dismissed between 2:30 and 3:30 p.m. This staggered schedule allows groups to get to the program and settle in before the next group arrives. However, some schools release all students at the same time.

The afternoon schedule usually consists of a series of activities and the transitions between the activities. Programs vary in the amount of time that is spent in teacher-planned activities and in structured situations. In some programs activities and materials are available throughout the afternoon, and children choose what they want to do. Staff are assigned areas and activities to supervise, and the children move between them. In other programs specific activities are planned for certain segments of the day, and the children follow that plan. Many variations of the two kinds of structures can be used effectively.

Table 1

*Sample Schedules
for SAC Programs*

Before- and After-School Day

Before School:

7:00–8:00	Children arrive; do quiet activities, such as games, puzzles, or block play; or work on homework.
8:00–8:15	Time for cleaning up and gathering belongings for school.
8:15	Children leave for school; kindergartners walked to classroom.

After School:

11:30	Kindergartners picked up from classroom; things put in cubbies.
11:45–12:15	Outdoor active play, free play, or planned activity.
12:15–12:45	Clean up for lunch; eat lunch; clean up after lunch.
12:45–1:15	Planned activity for kindergartners (art, music, science, health, language or math-readiness games).
1:15–1:30	Story time.
1:30–2:00	Rest or quiet time.
2:00–3:00	Quiet activities for those who are awake; sleepers rise when ready.
3:00–3:30	Arrival and sign-in of older children.
3:30–4:00	Snack available; free choice of indoor activity and play areas or outdoor play.
4:00–4:15	Group-meeting and planning time; staff set up activities.
4:15–5:00	Planned activities, clubs, homework.

5:00–6:00	Activity cleanup; individualized activities, free play outdoors or in gymnasium; prepare to go home.
6:00	Center closes.

Extended Afternoon

2:00–2:15	All children in the program arrive at the same time, or children leave for a field trip.
2:15–2:30	Group-planning time.
2:30–3:00	Planned activities, clubs, projects, free-play choices.
3:00–3:15	Snack.
3:15–5:00	Planned activities, clubs, homework.
5:00–6:00	Activity cleanup; individualized activities, free play outdoors or in gymnasium; prepare to go home.
6:00	Center closes.

Full Day

7:00–9:30	Free choice of activity areas, games, and materials for self-directed artwork.
9:30–10:00	Snack available; clean up activity areas.
10:00–11:30	Planned activities, clubs, projects; free-play choices available.
11:30–12:30	Lunch and cleanup.
12:30–1:30	Rest or quiet activity.
1:30–3:00	Planned activities, clubs, long-term projects; free-play choices available.
3:00–3:30	Snack; group-planning time.
3:30–5:00	Planned activities, clubs, long-term projects; free-play choices available.
5:00–6:00	Cleanup; activity areas and materials available.

The schedule is similar to the full-day schedule, except that children who attend only the before- and after-school program need to be integrated into the full-day program. When the SAC program is on a school site, the schedule, particularly outdoor or high-noise-level activities, needs to be synchronized with the elementary school program to avoid disturbing children doing quiet work. The integration of children in after-school care begins at approximately 3:00 p.m., when the children are dismissed from the elementary school program and they rejoin the children in the year-round intersession program.

7:00–8:00	Snack and quiet time for both groups of children.
8:00–8:15	Cleanup; before- and after-school group leaves for elementary school.
8:15–3:00	Same as full-day schedule for children on intersession.
3:00–3:30	Children on intersession may do physical education or other recreational activities with part of the staff; after-school children come in and may do homework or other quiet activities.
3:30–4:00	Snack and group-planning time for the whole group.
4:00–5:30	Planned activities, clubs, projects; free-play choices available.

There are many transitions between activities throughout the afternoon. By early evening, as their work day finishes, parents pick up their children.

Extended Afternoon

When school closes early, children at all grade levels often arrive at the center at the same time, usually early in the afternoon. On those days more time is available for activities that take longer to finish, staff have the opportunity to offer more activities, and children have lots of time to relax if they wish. Many programs plan special projects or field trips so that the long after-noon is more enjoyable for both staff and children.

Full-Day Program

Many programs remain open during school vacations and holi-days year-round and operate full day. On those days the program often has a different feeling because children have more time to play and feel less rushed to take advan-tage of all possible activities, creating a more relaxed atmo-sphere. Many programs use the time for activities requiring a great deal of time and space, which may not be available during the regular school day. Special outings or field trips are also planned. The day is often far more casual, and the pace is slower.

Children enter the programs in the morning and move into low-key activities until planned activities are offered, usually by midmorning, at which time a snack is normally served. Children participate in planned or self-chosen activities until lunchtime. In some programs children eat lunch together, and in others children may group themselves in a variety of areas. During early afternoon some programs offer a quiet or rest period for younger children (or older ones who wish to rest). During the middle of the day, especially in areas in which the heat may be intense, many programs encourage children to engage in quieter activities, then move toward more active play as the afternoon progresses. On long days children can play games for which there is not usually time after school (such as a full nine-inning softball game or a game of Monopoly).

Year-round Program

More and more schools are changing to year-round calendars, in which the school is open all year long, because the schools are overcrowded and need to make the most efficient use of the facility. A year-round school calendar differs from the traditional school calendar in that the school does not close for the summer or during spring and winter breaks. On a year-round school calendar, two to three groups of children attend school while one group is on break (intersession). The breaks usually occur three times per

year. For example, one group of children would be on intersession in January, May, and September, and another group would be on intersession in February, June, and October.

The year-round school calendar has certain implications for SAC programs. One implication relates to the months of the year and the times of the day during which the SAC program is offered. With staggered intersessions there will always be some children who need full-day care. In addition, ongoing before- and after-school care will be necessary for the children who are on a traditional school calendar or who are attending a year-round school and are not on intersession.

The year-round school calendar also affects the typical SAC curriculum. Many children will be on intersession during the cold, rainy winter months when some program activities, such as swimming and certain field trips, will not be possible. More time is available for

long-term projects and community activities, such as scouts, 4-H, Little League, and swimming at the community pool. New and interesting activities for a full-day program and special activities, such as field trips, are spaced throughout the year.

How Are the Children Grouped?

There are many ways to group children in SAC programs. Some large centers have a group for each grade level; some have two or three groups of several grades or developmental levels; and some programs choose to work with all age groups together. Many programs take a combined approach and group children by developmental level for parts of the day (so that planned activities can be tailored to their needs) and offer activities for the whole group at other times. At those times children can form smaller subgroups according to their own interests and desires.

What Are the Benefits of Quality SAC Programs?

In an effective, well-planned program, you can expect to see children who are:
- Engaged
- Having fun
- Challenged
- Learning
- Self-confident
- Making friends

What Are the Characteristics of a Quality SAC Program?

An exemplary school-age care program must include certain characteristics drawn from the California Department of Education's *Exemplary Program Standards for Child Development Programs Serving Preschool and School-Age Children* (EPS), which defines indicators of quality for programs serving children ages three to fourteen years. Implementing those characteristics will help you and your staff develop an exemplary program through a process of continuous growth and improvement.

This program guide expands on the characteristics found in the EPS and groups them in the following categories: working with school-age children (five to fourteen years old), planning program activities, creating environments, managing the program, and establishing partnerships with parents, schools, and the community. Those categories will be discussed in the following chapters.

Chapter 2

Working with School-Age Children

In designing a school-age care program that meets the needs of the children, you need to make many decisions based on current theory and research about how children grow and learn. The theoretical framework described in this chapter holds that a school-age care program should be developmentally and culturally appropriate as well as appropriate for the individual needs of the school-age child. The framework addresses school-age children's cognitive, social-emotional, physical, creative, and ethical development, providing a basis for decision making and positive interactions.

How Children Grow and Develop

An interactionist, constructivist theoretical framework is appropriate in considering school-age care. This approach emphasizes that children grow and learn through their interactions with other children, adults, and materials in the environment (Piaget 1976). The children gather information and develop concepts by becoming actively involved with what they are doing. When they are fully involved, they learn more about the particular activity and build more complex concepts and ideas through enriched experiences.

The children gather information and develop concepts by becoming actively involved with what they are doing.

Children further shape their concepts and attitudes as they continue to observe, question, form opinions, and test and reevaluate their conclusions. They construct their own ideas through problem solving and make decisions based on real-life experiences. This sort of learning can occur naturally in a school-age care program when activities are planned so that the child is wholly involved in the program in a relaxed, fun manner. The children are given opportunities to learn and develop fully.

Another commonly accepted theory is that children's thinking and logic change and develop in stages and that at least three different stages of thinking evolve between five and fourteen years of age (Piaget 1965). In each stage the child is able to grasp more complicated concepts than in the stage before, and each stage is reached only when the previous stage has been mastered. This growth in thinking and logic also affects the child's social and moral development. For example, how a child thinks and relates to his or her peers or thinks about the rules of a game or sport is related to the child's level of thinking and problem-solving ability.

Young children are not able to hold several concepts in their mind at one time and do not necessarily see the interrelatedness of certain ideas. Their thinking is illogical from an adult's perspective. As children move to the next stage, their thinking becomes more logical, but they must have concrete materials to manipulate in order to understand the concepts. Most older children then enter the third stage, which involves more abstract hypothetical thinking.

The children in a SAC program may be at different stages of intellectual development because of the wide range of ages often found in the program. Staff must provide activities that are open-ended to accommodate all those levels. Because the children usually work in mixed age groups, the younger ones also grow and learn naturally from their peers (Katz 1990).

Recent ground-breaking research into human intelligence by Howard Gardner has changed how psychologists view intelligence and human potential (Gardner 1993). Some of Gardner's findings are that people have the ability to improve and expand their intelligence; that intelligence can change and be taught to others; and that there are many intelligences, not just one. Furthermore, different cultures value different intelligences and may cultivate those intelligences more than others. Intelligence appears to come in many forms, and each child has strengths in different areas. Americans have traditionally considered intelligent those children who have the ability to do well in academic areas, such as language arts, science, and mathematics. However, children who do well in other areas, such as physical coordination and interpersonal skills, also exhibit valid forms of intelligence, and those are to be equally valued.

Children need experiences to capitalize on their own intelligences but also need to be provided with experiences that build on their other, less developed intelligences. SAC staff can use this information to be sure they are planning activities that will build on all kinds of intelligence and will help children to develop in areas that are less strong. For example, if an activity is planned that involves reading a play, some children might make the props, some might dance in the play, and some might prepare the musical accompaniment. All the children might eventually read parts of the play because the staff has first tapped into the children's particular intelligences before moving on to the linguistic aspect of reading the play.

While children are gaining intellectual understanding, they are also growing socially and emotionally. Children pass through several stages of social-emotional development on their way to adulthood (Erikson 1993). In the early school years, children become more independent of the adults in their lives and often feel some conflict about the changing nature of their relationship with those important adults. They are somewhat rigid in their views of right and wrong and look to adults for correct answers (Piaget 1965).

During this stage children need to be encouraged to make independent choices but need to know that adults are available to help them when necessary. Mastering skills intellectually, socially, physically, and creatively becomes a high priority. The children become aware of differing points of view and must learn to make rational social decisions in their games and work. To develop positive self-concepts, they need to experience success in developing those skills. SAC programs can assist children by providing a wide variety of activities at different levels of difficulty so that all children can experience success.

School-age children are also developing ethically (Piaget 1962; *Moral* 1991). They go through stages of development in which they learn social rules and ethics. They learn about sportsmanship, fair play, sharing, and taking turns. They may also develop civic and democratic values. As children grow older, they are able to evaluate social issues critically and become willing to change injustices. Children need the opportunity to talk and discuss freely issues that are important to them. They need opportunities to "step into the shoes" of other people to understand others' points of view. SAC programs can provide those opportunities through group discussions and role-playing and by talking through children's disagreements on the spot.

Children need plenty of time for free play as part of their physical development.

Physical development is another high priority in SAC programs. Children in the programs have many opportunities for free play as well as for organized sports and games. Learning to move and learning through movement are fundamental to the development of the child's self and social skills and to the child's experiences with the physical environment. Regular physical activities help the children remain healthy and happy. Children with special needs must also be given opportunities to expand their physical development to their limits. The children in SAC programs have many opportunities to participate in a variety of physical activities, such as basic movement skills, physical fitness, rhythm and dance, games, sports, tumbling and gymnastics, swimming, and outdoor education. Many SAC programs include some community activities, such as swim-

ming at the local pool, as part of their regular schedule; in the summer an all-day SAC program may even have opportunities for camping.

Children need plenty of time for free play as part of their physical development. They also need time for fun and relaxation. Children enjoy playing and want to spend time in such activities (Baldwin 1993). Moreover, learning takes place during free play. Free play for children involves spontaneous planning and makes use of natural materials; it is creative, deeply absorbing, and highly sensory. Such play allows children to play through their ideas and is an approach to problem solving (Van Hoorn and Nourot 1992). Symbolic or pretend play is also related to creativity and imagination.

For younger school-age children, spontaneous and make-believe play is common; for older children, action projects involving more realistic props are a kind of play. Playful activity, both organized and free, is a natural part of SAC programs. Play is a way of integrating all areas of development, including cognitive, social, physical, creative, and ethical development. See Table 2 for a summary of the stages of play for school-age children.

A child's physical development is also related to his or her overall personal health (*Health Framework* 1994). Promoting a child's health and well-being is part of the SAC program. Children learn to accept personal responsibility for their health by realizing they have some control over it. SAC programs are encouraged to collaborate with health and social service agencies to promote the health of the children in the program.

Table 2
Stages of Play

Young Child *(about five through seven years old):*

- Uses toy replicas of objects for dramatic play; begins to use unstructured props, such as blocks

- Creates imaginary playmates and engages in solitary fantasy play

- Begins to understand someone else's point of view

- Becomes more involved in socially oriented play

- Plays games with little regard for the rules

Older Child *(about eight through ten years old):*

- Can use symbolic props but prefers real objects in dramatic play

- Engages in socially oriented cooperative play

- Is able to understand others' viewpoints

- Plays games with rules correctly

- Can play team sports

Oldest Child *(about eleven through thirteen years old):*

- Creates dramatic roles and situations without costumes or props

- Writes, produces, and performs in sophisticated plays

- Understands others' points of view, including those of people from other times and places

- Becomes involved in highly developed cooperative play

- Engages in highly organized games with rules; changes illogical rules

The visual and performing arts play an extensive role in the creative development of children. Visual and performing arts include the multisensory disciplines of dance, drama/theater, music, and art (*Visual and Performing Arts Framework* 1989). Most SAC programs offer some kind of art project every day and encourage children to choose one or more of the activities daily. The youngest children in the program usually like to explore the art medium. Older children often like to analyze their own growth and skill in their creative projects. They might even want to have an art exhibit at the end of the program. These creative approaches encourage children to interact with their environment and learn to understand it. Children are given the opportunities to experience, create, analyze, and reorganize their experiences in ways that make sense to them. Children can draw on all their intelligences, including their musical and bodily kinesthetic ones, through the visual and performing arts (Gardner 1984).

Consideration must be given to integrating the child's cultural and family values into the program. Children need to develop the ability to be comfortable and work effectively in a pluralistic society, especially in California, with its rapidly changing demographics. Providing culturally responsive care is an ongoing learning process for adults and children as they learn about their own cultures and the cultures of other people (Derman-Sparks 1989). To learn about new people and cultures, children (and adults) must first

acknowledge that cultural differences and similarities exist; be willing to ask for information about the other person's beliefs and values—and listen nonjudgmentally; then be willing to adapt their behavior to deal with the new understanding. They need to use skills such as problem solving, negotiating, and communicating. With the staff's help, children need to develop a feeling of "groupness" and an ability to see the perspectives of others in order to prepare for a multiethnic future (Cortez 1991).

Bridges need to be built between a child's home and school cultures when those are different. The SAC program needs to include the child's culture, values, and primary language, and one of the best ways to do that is by involving the parents and community. SAC programs, with their flexible structure, allow for a great many cultural and community-based experiences, including discussions, field trips, guest speakers, parental sharing, and group projects that allow children to learn about and appreciate people who are both like and different from themselves. Such projects also help children learn about themselves. Cultural understanding and appreciation can take place in a way that integrates understanding into the regular program activities.

In summary, SAC programs have the opportunity to provide a great deal more than a safe place for children to be when they are not in school. The programs can enhance children's lives by supporting their intellectual, social-emotional, physical, creative, and ethical development through educational and recreational means. Program decisions and planning should reflect a knowledge of the possibilities presented by an interactionist and constructivist theory of active learning. Understanding how children can grow and develop optimally in SAC programs will become clear as you read about the program's characteristics and the activities suggested in this guide. By participating in SAC programs, children can grow in their understanding of the world, in their appreciation of themselves and others around them, and in their ability to become healthy and productive members of their generation.

Needs of School-Age Children

To be effective, school-age care programs must be designed to meet the needs and interests of the children the programs serve. Therefore, identifying and understanding those needs is a crucial skill for the staff in SAC programs. Decisions about curriculum planning, behavior management, environmental design, and program policy must be based on an awareness of school-age children and how their particular needs can be met during out-of-school hours. There are several basic issues to examine when considering the effect of children's development on SAC programming.

Most SAC programs serve a range of grade levels, often covering the full scope of kindergarten through grade six and sometimes including grades seven and eight. That arrangement means that programs must plan activities and policies that will effectively meet the needs of five-year-old children as well as those of twelve-to-fourteen-year-old children. The levels of development vary in each age range. Therefore, for every group of children five to fourteen years old, you are dealing with abilities, social development, and physical maturity that reflect a much wider age range. That reality is especially significant when you are serving children whose developmental and ability levels are far different from those of the other children in their age group.

In addition, some staff may have a tendency to assume that they can categorize and understand a child by virtue of his or her chronological age or that they can categorize a child as generally more or less mature than others of the same age. But each child is a combination of developmental levels, which may include some levels that are far advanced for the child's chronological age and some levels that are similar to those of much younger children.

The child whose intellectual development appears to be average for his or her age may be socially well advanced but have poorly developed physical skills and coordination. Each child must be viewed as the sum of his or her various developmental levels and as a unique person. Differences in culture and language, family background, learning modality strength, personality style, and personal history combine to make each child a special and unique person with individual hopes, dreams, thoughts, fears, and strengths. To enable children to appreciate themselves and others for their special qualities, staff must recognize and reinforce the value of each child.

Developmental Stages of School-Age Children

Children in school-age care programs can be divided into three basic age groups: younger, older, and oldest. Children in the different age ranges will exhibit different behaviors, ways of thinking, and interests. When you understand more about the different developmental stages, you can plan your program activities more effectively.

Younger School-Age Children

The younger children, about five through seven years of age, generally are in kindergarten through second grade. They are found in SAC programs in the greatest numbers and often have the largest effect on planning. Many staff view the younger children as the easiest group with which to work because they are still attached to teachers and often have developed fewer of the challenging behaviors that are typical of older

children. Although their thinking is egocentric, younger children love to initiate many different activities and are eager to learn. They will ask a thousand questions, so SAC staff should take advantage of their wonderful curiosity and this imaginative period. This group has its own special needs, which can easily be overlooked in the presence of older, more articulate children.

Older School-Age Children

The children in this age group are approximately eight through ten years of age and, usually, are in grades three through five. This period is an important transitional time for many children because they are moving from being "little kids" toward being teenagers. The staff can work with the children in this age group on some exciting projects because the children are hardworking and like to do something realistic. The children are beginning to think logically and understand how things work. They are forming vital perceptions about themselves and the world and are developing critical attitudes about school success, gang participation, and drug experimentation.

However, these children, like the middle children in some families, run the risk of receiving less attention in the pressure on staff to take care of the immediate needs of younger children and to deal with the challenges of older children's struggles to become independent. It is important that programs maintain an awareness of the middle children and support them in making a smooth transition through this period in their lives.

Oldest School-Age Children

Many programs find that the most challenging group comprises the oldest children, those who are about eleven through thirteen years old in grades six through eight. Many preadolescents pose a challenge to all the adults in their lives as well as to themselves. The period of time between childhood and young adulthood is one of tremendous physical and social change and upheaval for most children because, at this age, they are seeking to become more independent. Their physical growth and hormonal changes result in wide physical energy and mood swings.

When your staff understand and accept those changes, they can capitalize on the high energy and empathize with the changing moods. You can talk with the children in depth because they are able to think abstractly and are becoming idealistic. You must approach them with a somewhat different mind-set than you do with younger children. If you understand the developmental stages and unique needs of children in this age group, it will be much easier to provide an appropriate and enjoyable program that is particularly suited to them.

Programs for Different Age Ranges

It is important that staff enjoy, respect, appreciate, and understand children at each of the different developmental stages. By understanding more about each stage, staff will be able to plan effective programs that capitalize on the strengths and special features of each age range. The chart titled "Developmental Stages of the School-Age Child" (see Appendix A) contains information about typical needs and behaviors of children in the three basic age groups and suggestions for effectively interacting with them. In reviewing the chart, be aware that in each stage some children will exhibit behaviors of previous or later stages of development. Do not depend completely on the information for a specific age; instead, think of the stages as general ways of considering approximate age groups. You need to understand also that children move from one stage to another gradually, not in one jump that is consistent across all areas of development.

Use the information in the chart to plan appropriate activities, choose effective methods of discipline and guidance, and structure the schedule and flow of your program to meet the wide variety of needs and stages represented within your group of children. You may even want to group the children according to the three basic age ranges. Be creative in finding ways to provide the kind of adult intervention, level of challenge, and peer interaction the children need. By considering the developmental needs of children in planning, you can design a program in which the participants are happier and more excited, the staff enjoy and feel fulfilled by their work, and the parents appreciate the activities and environment you provide for their children. The program activities suggested in Chapter 3 were planned with the three basic developmental stages in mind.

Positive Interpersonal Interactions

Children learn a great deal from listening to the adults around them. Staff need to be aware of their interactions with the children and other staff members so that the messages they send are the ones intended. Because the words used in a conversation are a relatively small percentage of the actual communication, staff members should be aware of the tone of voice, facial expression, and body language they employ. The following principles are important in creating effective interactions in any SAC program.

Conversations with children contribute a great deal toward the children's learning and socialization. Staff should try to engage children in two-way conversations by showing sincere interest in children's ideas and opinions and through using such techniques as open-ended questions and active listening. Staff should also be aware that they are modeling language skills through their own speaking style; therefore, their language should be grammatically correct, and the subject matter of their conversations should be developmentally appropriate for the age of the children. Staff must also consider the differences in language and conversational style of all children, including those whose first language is not English, and understand the differences in the verbal and nonverbal messages of children from other cultures.

The feeling of being valued by others has a powerful impact

on the development of children's self-esteem. Children receive strong messages about how they are viewed and accepted by adults through both verbal and nonverbal communication. Their feelings of being valued and valuable are directly related to the children's perception of adults' attitudes and behaviors toward them. Therefore, staff need to be aware of the many ways in which their attitudes about children are communicated. Staff behaviors, such as showing respect for all children as individuals, acceptance and appreciation of cultural diversity, fairness and consistency in enforcing policies, empathy for children's feelings, and patience during stressful times, tell children that they are appreciated and valued by that adult. By modeling care and concern for others, staff help children develop a strong sense of self. Children need to be taught also how to stand up for themselves and each other. Establishing clear and consistent expectations for positive interactions between children and adults helps children acquire those skills.

Maintaining confidentiality is another key issue in communicating with school-age children. To be trusted and have credibility with children, staff members need to keep a child's conversations private unless the child allows the staff member to tell someone or unless what the child says indicates that he or she is in danger or that someone else is in danger. Repeating without permission what a child tells a staff person destroys that staff member's trustworthiness in the child's eyes.

Staff must also be aware of confidentiality in talking about children with other staff. Children are interested in conversations between staff and often overhear and pay attention to them, even though the adults may be unaware of the children's presence. It is important that staff do not discuss children's or parent's behavior, confidential information, or inappropriate subjects in any area in which children may be present.

Responsibilities in Supervising Children

Possibly the largest, and certainly the most crucial, part of any SAC person's job is supervising the children for whom he or she is responsible. The first priority for every frontline staff person is active supervision of children. Staff members need to spend a majority of their time supervising the children and must remember to properly observe the entire group for which they are responsible.

The following are some basic elements of SAC supervision that must be considered by all frontline staff. An example of a SAC program situation follows the description of the supervisory responsibility.

Choosing the Appropriate Level of Participation

The director of the program should make clear to the staff what level of participation is appropriate for specific activities. Some games and activities will require direct and constant involvement and will not allow the staff person to watch other areas at the same time.

Repeating without permission what a child tells a staff person destroys that staff member's trustworthiness in the child's eyes.

For other kinds of activities, the staff person just needs to be nearby to keep an eye (and ear) on the proceedings and be ready to step in if needed by the children. If teachers who are assigned to supervise an entire playground become too involved in one activity, they may be unaware of what takes place in other areas, and problems may result.

There are only two staff members on the playground with a lot of children. Several children want one of the adults to play four-square with them, but the other staff person is already involved in acting as referee for a large kickball game. If both adults are directly involved in a game, no one will be available to move around the playground to keep an eye on all the other activities. The adult needs to explain to the children why he or she cannot participate in the four-square game at that time. The person could say that if the children still want to play four-square the following day, he or

she could play with them while the other adult supervises the playground.

Being Aware of Each Child's Needs

SAC staff need to be aware that each child is an individual with unique needs, abilities, and interests. Staff should also realize that a child's needs often change as the child's home situation, health, developmental level, or perceptions change. Staff need to be aware of those changes in order to identify problems as they arise. Keeping in close touch with children's parents and classroom teachers will help staff to be aware of new developments in children's lives and can lead to a team approach in helping each child, as needed.

James has always been a cooperative and easygoing child, but lately he has been getting into fights and he cries easily. Giving him time-out for fighting seems to make things worse. You talk to his classroom teacher, who says that James has recently become very distracted and is not bringing in his homework. When you talk to his mother about the problems, she reveals that she and her husband have been arguing a lot lately and are talking about separating. Knowing this, you are able to redirect James when he has a difficult time and provide extra emotional support when he needs it.

Looking for Patterns of Problem Behavior

Another important supervisory responsibility is to look for patterns in children's behavior that can help identify possible causes when problems occur and find effective ways to deal with the problems. Take note of such circumstances as the time of day, the other children or adults involved, the environment, the program schedule, or the type of activity in which the child is participating and look for conditions that may be contributing to the problem. Try to find ways to manage the situation to produce the desired behaviors.

You find that there are a lot of fights and arguments in your program most days between 3:30 and 4:00 p.m. You serve snacks at 4:15 p.m. and realize that the children may be getting hungry and irritable before they receive their snacks. You try serving snacks at 3:45 p.m. for a week and discover that the number of fights drops dramatically.

Identifying the Cause of the Problem

When identifying problem behaviors, staff should sincerely ask themselves who is having the problem: Is the problem caused by the staff or the child? Are the staff's expectations for the child's behavior realistic, and have those expectations been clearly communicated to the child? Sometimes, what seem to be problems are the result of inappropriate expectations for school-age children outside the classroom setting.

Mrs. Thompson is an aide who works in a classroom during the school day and in the SAC program after school. She spends a lot of time and energy correcting children who do not stay in their seats until everyone has finished the snack. When the staff change the way that snacks are served and allow children to move on to other activities of their choice once they have cleaned up after their own snack, both the children and Mrs. Thompson are much happier at snack time.

Helping Children Make Choices

A major goal in working with children is to teach them to make good choices about their behavior. Children need to be able to identify reasons for behaving appropriately. It is important to recognize children for choosing to be cooperative, kind, helpful, and responsible and to show appreciation in a way that is consistent with the program's philosophy. Modeling appropriate behavior is also a powerful way of helping children learn to make good choices. Instead of moving in to provide solutions to children's conflicts, teachers should verbally demonstrate the steps involved in identifying the problem, generating options for resolving the problem, and choosing positive ways to help each child get some of what he or she wants. Children will begin to see that the process is an effective way to resolve problems and start using the techniques themselves. Staff need also to recognize the children's efforts and provide positive reinforcement for that kind of problem solving.

Mr. Martinez, a staff member, walks up to a small group working on an art project. Two of the children in the group had been arguing over who had the glue bottle first. One child had pulled it quickly from the other child, and the glue had spilled on the table. Mr. Martinez says, "What happened here? What is the problem?" He gives each child the opportunity to say what happened. Then he asks, "How can we solve this problem of having only one glue bottle to use? Are there any others available?" He also asks, "How will you clean up the spilled glue?" When they solve that problem, he asks, "How can we avoid this in the future?" Finally, he says, "You sure did a great job of solving this problem together."

The responsibilities outlined above are basic to supervising children in SAC programs.

Supervision also involves dealing effectively with behavioral problems as they arise. When staff members understand a child's developmental needs, family situation, school experience, and personal style, they will be able to choose appropriate behavior management techniques and activities for that child and effectively supervise all children in the group.

Behavior Management Techniques

SAC staff have to deal with a wide variety of behavioral problems on a day-to-day basis. The nature of children's developmental stages sometimes causes school-age children to act in ways that are trying for even the most knowledgeable and experienced person. Often, what staff perceive as inappropriate behavior is the result of children's natural desires to get attention or develop their independence. That does not always lessen the fact that such behavior can disrupt the program or present a danger to the children; therefore, that behavior must be discouraged.

Staff need to be aware of and comfortable with several behavior management techniques, and these techniques should be covered in the staff training. See Table 3, Behavior Management Techniques, for a list of techniques and examples of when and how to use them. Staff should be familiar with all of them and be willing to choose among them to meet the needs of any situation.

The severity of consequences of the selected technique needs to

Table 3
Behavior Management Techniques

	Situation	Solution
Offering sufficient and appropriate choices	At all times	Offer a wide variety of activities that interest children and create opportunities for success.
Modeling desired behavior	At all times	Demonstrate the kind of behavior that you would like to see from children, such as fairness, politeness, and cooperation.
Reinforcing appropriate behavior	Whenever possible	Use a variety of methods, such as acknowledgment, encouragement, or group rewards, that are consistent with the philosophy of your program. Build bridges to intrinsic rewards, particularly with older children, by saying, "How do *you* feel when you make the right choice?" In that way the child becomes self-motivated.
Staying in close proximity	When misbehavior is not serious but could become so if not addressed	Move to stand near the child so that he or she is aware of your presence.
Redirecting behavior	When minor behavior problems can be stopped by moving the child from the situation before the behavior escalates	Move the child to a new activity or area that will interest him or her and avoid the problem situation.
Discussing the problem and possible solutions	When a problem arises between children	Involve the children or the whole group in verbal problem solving or conflict resolution through discussing or role-playing possible solutions.
Giving verbal reminders	When a child is acting in opposition to the rules or policies of the center but is not creating an immediate danger to others or to the facility	Give one verbal reminder of the specific rule that was broken and the consequences agreed on earlier for continuing the behavior.
Using time-in	When a child continues acting in opposition to the rules after receiving a verbal reminder	The staff person who saw the behavior intervenes and tells the child that he or she has earned *time-in* (i.e., a specific amount of time) because the child again has broken the rule. The child stays with the staff person during the designated time. They discuss the broken rule and possible options for how to handle this situation in the future. When the time is over, the child goes back to the group.
Removing privileges	When a child has continued in opposition to the rules after receiving a reminder and using time-in	Restrict the child from participating in an activity that is related to the broken rule or provide other consequences that have been predetermined.
Arranging follow-through with parents	When techniques above have not resulted in an improvement in the child's behavior	Arrange for daily communication between the staff and parents and set up a positive behavior chart for each day (based on changed behavior in the SAC program). The SAC staff look out for the child "doing it right" throughout the day and verbally reward the child for doing so. Parents follow up at home with what they feel are appropriate consequences. The SAC staff may help the parents set up positive behavior reinforcement charts for the home.
Developing a contract	When other methods have produced little change in serious behavioral problems	Create a written agreement between the program, the parent, and the child, requiring specific levels of behavior for the child's enrollment in the program to continue.
Excluding from the program	When a child presents a real danger to other children or staff even after other methods have been tried	Inform parents that they must find new arrangements for care within a specified time frame. You might try to help them locate a different type of care that will work better for their child.

Note: The techniques above the dotted line are the more positive techniques and should be used on a regular basis. The methods below the line are to be used when a serious problem arises or one that might cause a danger to the children involved. The downward order indicates the increasing seriousness of the method and which method should be used first. Exclusion from the program should be used only when all other behavior management techniques have failed.

match the seriousness of a child's misbehavior and developmental level. Staff members should not let their immediate feelings lead them to react to children's behavior by applying techniques with overly strong consequences. It is essential for *every* staff member to apply techniques and consequences consistently so that children are not confused by mixed messages.

The rules and policies that you ask children to follow should be as positive as possible and emphasize what one *can* do rather than what one *cannot*. For example, a rule such as "Don't hit, push, or pinch" can be changed to "We are kind and considerate to each other." "No running in the room!" can become "We walk in the room." It is helpful to enlist the children's participation in the development of rules and policies. They will be more willing to cooperate when they understand and contribute to the policy-making process.

It is important to recognize children for choosing to be cooperative, kind, helpful, and responsible and to show appreciation in a way that is consistent with the program's philosophy.

Children also need the opportunity to talk about ethical and social issues that have occurred so that problems, such as name calling, can be resolved together. You can discuss the problem in planned small-group discussions, meetings of the whole group, or on-the-spot discussions with the children involved. You might even role-play the problem with the children so that they can try different ways of solving the problem and examine the consequences of their different solutions. In this way the children begin to understand other people's points of view and learn more socially acceptable ways of solving their problems.

You will need to reevaluate the rules and policies occasionally to ensure that they continue to be appropriate and that you have not created too many to remember and enforce.

Children Under Stress

Many ongoing and short-term situations in children's lives strongly affect the children's behavior and needs in the SAC program. Children undergo serious stress in situations such as divorce, separation, economic hardship, substance abuse, moving, gang influence, child abuse, or academic pressure. During those times children will need extra understanding and guidance or referrals for outside services. The program should have a variety of agencies in its referral file to pass on to parents in time of need.

For some children the SAC program can be one of the most stable and enjoyable parts of their day. Programs should try to create a secure, comfortable environment by reducing staff turnover, creating successful experiences, eliminating stressful competition, and providing a homelike environment. Staff need to have a variety of techniques at their disposal to assist children through stressful periods in their lives. The staff should discuss and practice such techniques as active listening, problem solving, brainstorming solutions, and providing emotional support.

In addition, the SAC program should try to develop a structure for connecting with other school and community services to ensure that consistent messages are sent; for example, between the school program and the SAC program. Classroom teachers can provide useful information about children's behavior and the ways that they are trying to assist the children.

It is important to keep the channels of communication open with school staff, community workers, parents, and children so that children's problems can be identified and addressed effectively. Staff members should talk informally with parents as they see problems developing to discuss mutual ways to help the child. If staff can form an alliance between the home, school, and SAC program, the chances of helping children increase dramatically.

Staff should also be aware of policies for referring children who seem to have serious problems to other program staff, school-linked services, or community agencies.

Directors should make clear to staff what techniques are acceptable to use in providing that guidance. It is essential that staff be supplied with specific information about state-mandated guidelines for reporting child abuse.

Children with Special Needs

Quality school-age care programs for children without disabilities tend also to be quality programs for children with disabilities or children with special needs. Children with disabilities are children first. They exhibit more similarities than differences when compared with children of the same age. All children need to be treated with kindness and respect and given opportunities to play and learn. With planning, training, and support, your SAC staff can successfully mainstream many children with special needs.

Historically, limited options for child care have been available for these children. Now, the Americans with Disabilities Act (ADA) requires that programs make a reasonable effort to accommodate all children in their programs. Often, the children will function beautifully in your program with little or no adaptation in the administration of the program. In some cases facilities may need adapting and staff may need training to adequately meet the needs of children with disabilities. Planning to accommodate these children involves assessment of the children's needs, the program environment, and your SAC program offerings and preparations to ease the integration of children with special needs.

Assessing the Child's Needs

A thorough assessment of the particular child involved is important for the successful integration of a child with special needs into a SAC program.

Children need to be treated with kindness and respect and given opportunities to play and learn.

(A complete intake assessment that documents the strengths and needs of every child who applies will enable you to determine whether your SAC program is appropriate for the child, whether or not the child has special needs.) Communication with the parents and with the school will help you to assess whether your program can offer the child appropriate care. Teachers and administrators can share information about the strengths and needs of children with disabilities as well as explain the disability.

Include the following elements in your assessment of children who may need special services in your program:

1. Observations of the child: If possible, observe the child in his or her school environment or in other group settings to determine the child's ability to participate in those settings.

2. Conferences with parents and teachers: Discuss the child's background, health status, current interests, and needs and how those needs might be met in your program. Set goals for the child in the SAC program.

3. Documentation review: Examine documents, such as the "Parent Survey," "Individual Education Plan," and "Psychological Evaluation Report," for a better understanding of the child's needs.

When observing children, talking with parents and teachers, and reviewing documents, you will need to look for factors that indicate whether the child will be able to function safely and successfully in your SAC program and what you can do to assist the child. In assessing the extent of a child's special needs, consider the following attributes of the child:

- Ability to successfully complete transitions
- Level of communication
- Level of aggression toward self and others
- Behavior when fearful of new situations
- Food allergies or other health issue

You need also to determine the extent of supervision the child will require in the following areas:

- Level of assistance necessary for self-help and for participation in group activities
- Oversight of special medical needs and conditions
- Control of possible seizure activity

- Kind of behavior management techniques required

Assessing the Environment

The program environment should be one in which a child with special needs feels safe and comfortable. You can create an environment that is appropriate for the special needs of the children you are serving by ensuring easy physical access to many different activity areas and by providing materials and equipment that the children can get at and use as independently as possible.

Consider the following questions in assessing the physical environment of your program to determine whether it will meet the special needs of the child:

1. Will your program site allow the child safe access to a full range of program activities?
2. Will any features of the site present a danger to the child?
3. Are there obstacles to mobility, such as passages too narrow for wheelchairs to negotiate?
4. Is equipment that may be dangerous, such as sharp scissors or glass objects, accessible to children who cannot distinguish danger?
5. What additional materials, supplies, and equipment will help the child participate successfully in and feel a part of the program?

Equipment and supplies should be available in sufficient quantity and variety to meet the diverse interests and needs of all children in the program. To meet special needs, you may want to review your supplies with the following in mind:

- Size (e.g., provide larger crayons and pencils that will be easier to hold and manipulate)
- Storage (e.g., place materials so that children in wheelchairs or with other mobility differences can reach them independently)
- Developmental or skill level (e.g., include low-reading-level books on topics that will interest older children)
- Specialized materials (e.g., provide large-print books for visually impaired children)

When selecting equipment and supplies, try to ensure that the items are adaptable, as much as is possible, for all the children in the program to avoid stigmatizing or singling out the children with special needs. If a child needs expensive specialized equipment, such as a communication board or special computer, find out whether the equipment is available on loan from the child's day program or home before purchasing it.

Assessing Program Offerings

Examine the curriculum offered by your program to ensure that all children are able to participate successfully in activities that are enjoyable, interesting, and enriching and promote the children's self-esteem. Activities and materials should foster mastery of skills for children with special needs. Activities that require learning new skills may need to be analyzed, broken down, and taught in small steps. You may need to organize small-group and individual activities for children who cannot successfully participate in large-group activities. The activity choices offered should be varied and reflect an awareness of the developmental levels and interests of the children. Children should have opportunities to solve problems and get involved in hands-on activities.

Consider the following questions in examining your program structure regarding a child with special needs:

The activity choices offered should be varied and reflect an awareness of the developmental levels and interests of the children.

1. What goals should be set to meet the child's needs?
2. Can the program provide access to a range of activities that are appropriate to the child's developmental level and age level?
3. Will the level of structure in the program be appropriate and safe for the child?
4. Will there be a positive environment in which the child can socialize and build self-esteem?
5. Is the SAC program flexible enough to adapt and make changes, if necessary, to meet the needs of the child?
6. How will the SAC staff prepare the children in the program for

the arrival of the child with special needs to ensure a smooth, accepting transition to the program?

Preparing for Children with Special Needs

One of the greatest barriers to successfully integrating children with special needs into SAC programs is the attitude of staff, parents, and other children in the program. An important step in making your program "special-needs friendly" is to educate and train the staff. Staff members may need further knowledge about a specific need or disability and training to care responsibly for the child. (Training to work with children with disabilities is discussed in Chapter 5, "Managing Your Program.") The following questions will help you evaluate staff skills for working with children with special needs:

1. Are staff members committed to serving children with special needs?
2. Will there be sufficient staff to provide the level of supervision needed by a particular child?
3. Are staff members available who are trained or open to training in disability awareness and care?
4. Will the staff act as appropriate role models for other children in dealing with the child's special needs?
5. Is the staff prepared to assess the child on a regular, ongoing basis to determine what is working and what is not working for the child?

After considering the child's particular physical or developmental challenge, you need to develop a plan for the child's transition to your program. Before the child with a disability joins your group, set a positive tone by openly and sensitively discussing the disability and educating the other children and parents. Explain the child's special needs clearly and honestly. Let the children and parents know that they will not "catch" the disability. By modeling an accepting and respectful attitude, staff can help children and parents develop nonbiased feelings toward children who happen to be different.

In addition, staff should encourage interaction between chil- dren with special needs and other children in the program to develop all children's social skills and awareness of others. Teachers must set the ex- ample of acceptance and appreciation of the similarities and differences between children, setting the tone for children to follow. Basically, the con- siderations discussed in this section are the same for all children in SAC programs, but children with special needs may have a greater range and diversity of needs.

Working with Parents

Providing all possible support and assistance for a child's family is an important aspect of helping any child. Parents who feel competent and relaxed in their own roles are better able to play the primary role in sup-

porting and teaching their children. To serve children with special needs adequately, the SAC program staff must include plans for involving and assisting parents and guardians. For example, the children may require special transportation to reach your center. If your program does not provide transportation, assist the parents in finding resources to meet that need. You can also refer parents of children with special needs to programs sponsored by community organizations and support groups that deal with the child's specific problem.

Inform parents of children with special needs that you are interested in being included in the Individual Education Plan (IEP) process because the parents can invite whomever they believe would be helpful. SAC staff may be invited to attend the informative IEP meetings in which a collaborative team discusses such matters as developmental goals, safety issues, and behavioral concerns. The SAC staff's participation in that process is to discuss the staff's observations of the child's development and progress in the SAC setting and learn ways to support the IEP.

Finding Additional Help

A number of outside resources are available to you. Your local child care resource and referral agency and the National Information Center for Children and Youth with Handicaps in Washington, D.C.,

offer information on special needs. Other agencies provide supportive services, including brochures, advice, and training in special needs. Be sure to get on the mailing list of organizations that serve the kinds of special needs with which you deal and pass along any information you receive to the appropriate parents. Assist parents, whenever possible, in gaining access to any available subsidy funding. Contact local agencies that specialize in providing services for people with special needs, such as the California Council for the Blind, California Department of Rehabilitation, the Easter Seal Society, and developmental disability centers. The Special Education Department of your school district and the Special Education Division, California Department of Education, also provide information and resources.

Including children with disabilities in the SAC program tends to be a humanizing experience for both adults and children. The group needs to work together in a cooperative way to solve unique daily challenges. When everyone cooperates, misunderstandings and misconceptions can be minimized or eliminated, and the program and everyone involved is enriched. This guide strongly supports a commitment among staff in SAC programs to include children with special needs so that the inclusion of such children becomes a natural consideration for the program.

Chapter 3

Planning Program Activities

Keeping the children involved in constructive and entertaining activities is a cornerstone of every SAC program. Much time and energy need to go into planning, facilitating, and cleaning up after the children's activities. But first you need to consider what you are trying to accomplish by including certain activities in your program. This chapter provides examples of many different activities related to a variety of purposes.

Determining the Purpose of Your Activities

One basic reason for planning activities is to keep children constructively engaged while they are in your care. When children are involved in games or activities, they have an ideal opportunity to talk, listen, cooperate, negotiate, lead, follow, and otherwise interact with other children and adults. A unique strength of SAC programs is the opportunity for children to work and play with children from different age groups. While they are in school, they may be segregated by age and deal mostly with children in their own grade level. SAC programs allow children to create their own "neighborhoods" or clubs in which older and younger children must learn to interact effectively to accomplish their goals. The older children learn to nurture and teach the younger ones, who, in turn, learn to cooperate and become valuable team members.

Well-planned activities allow children to learn and practice such skills as reading and writing, which may help the children be more successful students. Other abilities, such as critical thinking and scientific reasoning, are learned readily through activities that engage children's interest with hands-on experiences and interactions. Physical education skills can be developed through games, tournaments, and free play. Although SAC activities should not mirror school-day activities, experienced SAC professionals know that many concepts and skills that are important to children's success in school can be strengthened in fun and interesting ways outside of school.

Children also learn through play to act out some symbolic

representations, including pretending to be adults and trying out adult work. SAC programs are able to offer many fun ways to learn. If children are fascinated by a particular activity, project, or topic, they can spend days or weeks on that interest without getting off schedule.

One of the joys of working with school-age children is that they bring a wealth of good ideas to SAC programs. With adult guidance they can learn to brainstorm ideas, consider practical limits, and plan the execution of a wide variety of projects and activities. Including children's ideas and interests into SAC curricula is important in developing a responsive and effective program. However, because the purpose of SAC programs is to meet children's needs, staff must remember that sometimes children change their minds. What they planned and were excited about last week may not sound as interesting this week. Staff must avoid turning child-directed activities into teacher-directed activities by sticking inflexibly to old plans in the face of new possibilities.

The suggestions that follow will help you plan your program and achieve your purposes.

Planning Ahead

Some of the most enjoyable and memorable activities that occur in after-school programs come from spontaneous ideas and situations; but an effective program of activities usually requires dedicated planning and forethought. By planning ahead, you are able to purchase adequate supplies, schedule staff and facilities appropriately, and prepare children and parents for upcoming events. There are several important elements to consider in developing your curriculum and in choosing activities.

A crucial step is to determine the needs and interests of the particular group of children in your program. You can do that by observing how the children function in your program; by talking to them about their needs, interests, and hobbies; by asking the parents (through an interview or questionnaire) about their children's needs; and by talking to the children's elementary teachers. Children's needs differ, based on the child's age, gender, abilities, special needs, background, and expectations.

One of the joys of working with school-age children is that they bring a wealth of good ideas to SAC programs.

Consider issues such as the child's current interests, academic strengths and deficiencies, need for structure, and cultural and family values. Use all the information sources available to you, including parents, staff observations, elementary teachers, and the children themselves.

Too often, the interests and expertise of staff members are underutilized in planning activities. Staff may have hobbies or interests that translate well into activities that children enjoy. Projects involving handicrafts, woodworking, cooking, sports and games, or music, which

Children benefit by being able to consider their choices, thus generating excitement about upcoming events.

staff often pursue for their own recreation, can be used successfully in the after-school program. Calling on staff members to share their skills builds the staff's professional self-esteem and provides the program with enthusiastic activity leaders. Use your knowledge of the staff's hobbies, brainstorm sessions at staff meetings, or develop questionnaires to identify possible areas of interest.

For example, you might ask at a staff meeting whether anyone plays an instrument that can be taught to the children or played for them or used in background music for a SAC performance. Some staff members will need support and encouragement as they begin developing plans to create successful experiences for the children and themselves. Once accomplished, those planning skills add a valuable new resource to your program.

Staff should be involved regularly in evaluating and refining activities. One method is to keep a staff log to record reactions to each activity and suggestions for improvement. You might also include a discussion of activities from the past week or month as a regular agenda item in staff meetings. Try various methods of involving staff in planning and you will reap the benefits of enriched activities and staff commitment to the program.

Planning ahead should be a regularly scheduled procedure with specific responsibilities assigned to individual staff members. If there is no deadline for a task, or if everyone thinks that someone else will do it, the job may not get done. When staff are responsible for a particular activity for a given time period, they need to know well in advance what they need to submit as well as when and to whom they should submit it. Publishing and distributing or displaying plans at regular intervals helps the staff remember their duties and follow time schedules.

Once your plans for the upcoming week or month are finalized, post them for parents and children to inspect. For parents the posted plans will be a visible indication of the quality of your program. They often see only the quietest parts of the program in the early morning and late afternoon and may be unaware of the exciting activities that go on between those times. They can also plan for ways to contribute, such as by bringing in scrap materials or other items. Children benefit by being able to consider their choices, thus generating excitement about upcoming events. You may even wish to publish your plans in a newsletter;

provide a monthly calendar pictorially describing upcoming events; or send a flyer to people on your mailing list, which should include the local school principal, teachers, and your governing board members.

Some of the most disruptive yet least planned-for periods of the day are the times of transition between activities. Moving from outdoor active play to indoor group time or snack time can be a challenge, but you can ease the difficulty by planning for those transitions. Think about making an activity out of moving a large group of children from outdoors to indoors (such as a heel-to-toe walk) or using short activities to make the transition from active to quiet times (such as a game played while sitting on the floor in a circle). Other difficult times that can be eased through planning include temporary staff shortages, such as when two people call in sick at the last minute, or the arrival of children in a highly energetic state. Plans for those occasions should include a few activities that can be supervised in large groups or that children can play energetically but which require no special equipment and have simple rules.

It is important for children to participate in different kinds of group structures and activities. If all activities are planned for a large group, children never get a chance to participate in activities for smaller groups. Projects like woodworking or rocket building are difficult to supervise effectively with groups of 12 to 18 children. You can, however, offer that kind of activity to a small group of six to eight children during a concurrent large-group activity; for example, during a kickball game in which a staff member is effectively supervising many other children.

All activities need to be accessible to the girls as well as the boys in the program. For example, it should be expected that girls will do woodwork and rocket building and that boys and girls will play in the same kickball game if they choose to do so. However, boys and girls at this age often naturally break into same-sex activities, which they need to be allowed to do, too. But they need also to be encouraged to play or work together in various activities so that there is no gender stereotyping of activities and that opportunities for choices are equally available to boys and girls.

You should also provide a culturally responsive curriculum by integrating cross-cultural activities into the ongoing daily program. You need to include activities that support trust building and respect among children of different cultural and ethnic backgrounds. Avoid a "tourist" approach in which children learn only about the holidays, festivals, and costumes of other countries without internalizing and becoming sensitive to and appreciative of the similarities and differences among people. Encourage the sharing of family ethnic traditions, holiday celebrations, oral story telling, and cooking activities. Plan those activities as a natural, integral part of the curriculum; they should not be an add-on or afterthought.

Books, music, and games in the program should be current, culturally diverse, and nonstereotypic.

Provide materials and activities that affirm individual strengths, similarities, and differences in cultures. You can also add cultural richness to your program by sharing the varying experiences of staff, children, and parents and any community resources that are available. Staff will need to be open to discussing daily, on a natural basis, questions or issues raised by the children about racial or cultural concerns.

Books, music, and games in the program should be current, culturally diverse, and nonstereotypic.

Another wise decision is to plan for activities that can help the children in your program through traumatic situations, such as natural disasters, civil unrest, or large-scale accidents. In times of tremendous upheaval, children have many fears and questions that you should be ready to deal with through well-planned activities and professional volunteers. For example, an earthquake is a common California disaster for which many programs prepare, particularly in areas near fault lines. Programs usually prepare a big container of canned food and other supplies that can be used if an earthquake or other disaster hits the area. Children can help decide what will go into that survival kit. Develop a full disaster plan of action that includes specific responsibilities for each staff member as well as

emergency telephone numbers. Form disaster task groups and give each group a specific assignment in case of disaster. Practice procedures with the children and talk with them about natural disasters.

Prepare for crisis counseling, which should be available to the children, staff, parents, and community members who need it. Talk to parents about what behaviors to expect of children after a disaster occurs. Be aware that the children will need time to talk about the disaster and their feelings and reactions to it once it has occurred. Begin now to collect articles and suggestions from programs that have been through a disaster and keep them on file so that you will be prepared to act quickly if the need arises.

Involving Adults Appropriately

Staff who are used to working with preschoolers sometimes have difficulty adapting to appropriate adult involvement in school-age children's activities. In SAC programs the children are becoming increasingly independent, and staff must support that behavior but still provide the security of an adult nearby. Being available but not too intrusive is difficult for some adults. Several appropriate roles for adults in SAC programs are described on the following page.

Planners. One of the roles that staff play is to think ahead about fun activities that would improve children's lives. Even when children contribute to the planning, adults usually need to "get the ball rolling"—and nudge it now and then to keep it moving.

Encouragers. Another SAC staff role is to give extra praise and encouragement to those children who tend to say "I can't." However, staff must not go overboard in trying to get children to participate in activities in which they are truly uncomfortable. That will create more fear or defiance in the process. Encourage, do not force.

Facilitators. Staff act as facilitators by bringing all the materials and resources of a project together and taking care of the details to ensure that the project is successful. That can be an especially challenging task in SAC centers, in which so many things are happening at one time and the children have different needs and personalities.

Participants. Certain activities, such as card games or games of chance, are appropriate for staff to do along with the children, who enjoy seeing adults engage in the activities and may be stimulated by the staff's attention and enthusiasm. Staff participation can work well in situations that are not highly competitive or physically interactive, in which the adult's size or skill may cause frustration or potentially dangerous accidents. Projects in which the staff's completed work will outshine the children's work or projects that tend to make the children feel that the adult's way is "the" way to do it are also not appropriate for staff participation.

Observers. Supervision of children often involves standing back and keeping an eye on several groups or activities at one time to ensure that things are running smoothly and that no one gets hurt. That kind of observation allows staff to see potential problems as they arise or to learn more about individual children; but when staff are scheduled to be working with children, the staff need to focus their full attention on the children's actions and the flow of the program.

Instructors. Some projects involve explaining or demonstrating new skills or techniques that children need to complete the activity successfully. At those times it is important to keep basic instructional strategies in mind; for example, present clear and concise directions, ask questions to check for understanding, and reexplain in a different way for those who did not initially understand. Because each child learns most effectively in his or her own manner, through visual, auditory, or kinesthetic signals, staff should try to present the information in several ways (pictorial or demonstrated directions, verbal directions, and hands-on practice).

Collectors and providers of materials. The staff has to make sure that everything is collected and available at the appropriate time and place. The staff may also have to be creative about collecting things that will excite children, stimulate their creativity, or encourage their participation, such as unusual scraps for art projects or special equipment for games. The role of collector often involves being creative about identifying sources for obtaining materials at little or no cost; for example, through garage sales, parents' donations, local business donations, and cooperative arrangements with other centers to create toy banks.

"Firefighters." One of the least enjoyable yet most called-on roles of staff is to put out "fires" by taking care of arguments, accidents, emergencies, or other small and large crisis situations that arise when children play together. Knowing that an adult is nearby to help solve problems helps children develop the independence that is necessary as they mature.

SAC staff must operate in a kind of "rubber-band" manner, in which they move into children's activities to provide materials and get them started, then move back to observe, then move in to encourage continued effort in the face of frustration, then move back to observe, then move in when children cannot settle a problem on their own, and so forth. This in-and-out relationship and the ability to judge when children need their intervention are important skills for SAC staff to develop. The most successful staff are those who come in at the right time with enthusiasm and encouragement to get and keep projects and games moving but can wait that extra second to let children work out difficulties on their own before stepping in to help.

Ensuring Activities Are Developmentally Appropriate

Keep your children in mind when you are planning activities for them. The levels of development at which the children are challenged will determine the success or failure of each activity. People are often tempted to classify children by age or grade level and assume that the abilities and interests of children in one level will be similar. However, a child's combined age, skill, and maturity level may cause that child to be more like children outside his or her age group. That is particularly (but not solely) true of children with special needs because their disabilities may affect their development in a variety of ways. There are several issues to consider in planning activities that will match school-age children's developmental needs as much as possible.

Many activities can be adapted to make them more or less complex depending on the participants. Games may be played with rules or challenges that allow for various skill and ability levels, even when children with different skill levels are playing simultaneously. For example, a board game that requires answering questions can have cards with questions of varying difficulty. Try a system using A-B-C-D levels of difficulty from which the child can choose, depending on his or her comfort level. Large-group games, such as kickball, can be adapted to require less coordinated movements from less mature children, such as the option to kick the ball from a standstill rather than have the ball pitched, and let children choose their level of challenge.

Do not just assume that you know school-age children and plan for them according to your assumptions. You have a captive group at your disposal from whom you can learn, so ask what they would like to do. Plan some brainstorming sessions in which the children talk about what interests them, and the adults listen. Ask the children about the activities you have done in the past. Which activities do they remember? Which activities did they like, and which did they think were "stupid"? Brainstorming does not mean that the children completely plan the program, but it will give you many ideas about the kinds of activities that will be successful with your children and which ones will probably fall flat, even though they sounded great when you read about them in a book.

School-age children need much less structure and repetition in their activities than do preschool children. School-age children need opportunities to exercise their developing problem-solving ability, creativity, and curiosity. Sometimes they need to try new skills and techniques, even though the results are less attractive than you would like. Avoid projects that require only replication of a pattern or projects in which the adults contribute the major effort and the children add only a small part of the finished work. School-age children like to create individualized products, and staff goals should be to help the children appreciate the process. The way that a product looks when finished is not the most crucial part of the project; learning along the way is the goal. However, because older school-age children are more interested in the finished product and what it looks like, some of the more challenging projects could be multiday projects, community service projects, or complex projects, such as putting on a play.

An important developmental need for school-age children is to feel that they are creating a useful product or providing a meaningful service. Older children usually rebel at doing projects that have the obvious goal of filling time, such as coloring or connecting dots. Projects are more enjoyable when real tools and materials are used rather than the miniature or less fragile ones that are often given to children. When children are not participating enthusiastically in an activity, look at its apparent goal. Do children see how the activity is relevant to themselves or the world? If not, you may need to rethink the project or find a better way to help children see how it fits into a larger project or skill. Consider doing the following activities:

- Creating art projects that will become part of a gift or a display at the center
- Writing stories to produce a book to share with younger children
- Studying pictures of airplanes if you will soon be building a rocket

Children have a difficult time seeing complex relationships and internalizing and adapting new information to existing concepts without active involvement. They need a lot of concrete interaction and examples of how to process information. Create ways for children to interact with materials, people, and the environment so that they can figure out relationships and concepts through problem solving and trial-and-error discovery.

One of the big advantages of the wide range of ages in after-school programs is the opportunity for children to help each other. More mature children can help the younger members of their team succeed or teach skills and develop concepts that they themselves have recently learned, thus reinforcing their own learning. Older children enjoy the feeling of maturity instead of being treated as children themselves, and younger children usually enjoy the positive attention of older children. Include projects and activities that require extra cooperation between different groups of children and encourage their efforts with suggestions or demonstrations of how goals can be achieved and participants can be motivated.

Creating a Balanced and Integrated Program

A basic indicator of quality in SAC programs is the availability of a balanced selection of activities. A balanced program means that a number of different kinds of activities are offered to the children on a regular basis—no one or two kinds of activity dominate the program. Different activities are designed to enhance the cognitive, linguistic, social–emotional, ethical, physical, and creative development of each child (see Table 4). There is also a balance between small-motor and large-motor activities, active and quiet activities, and child-initiated and teacher-initiated activities. Activities are designed to meet children's different styles of learning and intelligence strengths as well as children's special needs. A balance between structured and nonstructured and between indoor and outdoor activities is also recommended.

When planning, review your upcoming activities to see whether any particular kind of activity seems to be over- or underrepresented. However, keep in mind that the areas often overlap and that one activity may offer several opportunities. Play activities often overlap or integrate other activities, such as those suggested in Table 4, by encouraging children to participate for the sake of having fun. Play activities may be planned or may happen spontaneously in an environment that stimulates children's imagination and offers space and time for free-play choices. You can examine some activities to determine whether they integrate several developmental areas at one time, depending on the focus of the activity (see examples in Table 5).

Planning integrated activities is important because these activities help school-age children understand the ways that things are interconnected and help children make sense of their world. To make sure that children's experiences and, therefore, growth are encouraged in as many ways as possible, examine your curriculum to see that it provides balance in group size (large, small, partners, and individual); activity level (active and quiet play); length of project (long term and short term); and play area (indoors and outdoors).

Table 4
Activities in a Balanced Program

Cognitive Activities

These activities stimulate children's thinking and intellectual abilities:

- Games and activities that reinforce academic skills and concepts
- Scientific experiments and projects
- Projects that require critical-thinking and decision-making skills

Language Development Activities

These activities reinforce children's skills in using words effectively in their primary or secondary language:

- Storytelling activities
- Activities that require reading or giving directions
- Word-based games, such as Scrabble or Password

Social–Emotional Activities

These activities provide opportunities for children to interact and learn more about each other and themselves:

- Games and activities that require teamwork and cooperation and build positive relationships
- Activities that focus in a positive way on similarities and differences among people and cultural values
- Activities that increase children's self-awareness and self-esteem

Ethical Activities

These activities help children critically examine their values and those of other people and groups:

- Role-playing of social or interpersonal problems that develop among the children
- Discussions to clarify or examine conflicting values or ethical beliefs among the children or between groups

Physical Activities

These activities provide children with opportunities to learn and strengthen small- and large-motor skills and coordination:

- Games or activities that encourage running, throwing, and other active play
- Projects that require fine-motor skills, such as cutting or lacing
- Activities that build strength and endurance, such as aerobics or physical fitness

Creative Activities

These activities encourage children to express themselves in nonprogrammed, imaginative ways by drawing inspiration from within themselves rather than from external models or directions. Some of the most frequently used creative activities involve the visual and performing arts, including:

- Art media, such as drawing, painting, or sculpting
- Music
- Drama
- Puppetry
- Creative writing
- Dance
- Integration of arts through a play, performance, or backyard circus

Table 5
Activities That Integrate Several Developmental Areas

Activity	Developmental Area					
	Cognitive	Linguistic	Social-Emotional	Physical	Ethical	Creative
Scrabble	x	x				
Dance			x	x		x
Fort building with blocks	x	x	x	x	x	x
Card game	x	x	x	x		
Role-playing	x	x	x	x	x	
Noncompetitive/ competitive games		x	x	x	x	

Integrative Activities

School-age care projects can integrate several curriculum and developmental areas and effectively involve a range of age groups. The curriculum areas referred to are drawn from the California curriculum frameworks for English–language arts, health, history–social science, mathematics, physical education, science, and visual and performing arts. The published frameworks describe the core curriculum for each subject or content area for kindergarten through grade twelve and provide direction for effectively transmitting the skills, knowledge, and understanding to the students. The activities suggested in this guide support in a fun way the concepts and skills that are presented in the frameworks and taught in the elementary and middle schools. The main goals for each subject are as follows:

English–language arts: To develop listening, speaking, reading, writing, and language skills and an appreciation of literature

Health: To accept responsibility for one's personal health; respect and promote the health of others; understand the process of growth and development; and acquire health-related information and knowledge of health products and services

History–social science: To gain cultural and historical knowledge; understand civic values and ethics; and develop social participation and critical-thinking skills

Mathematics: To learn numbers, measurement, geometry, pattern and function relationships, logic, and algebra

Physical education: To develop movement, personal, and social skills that encourage physical activity and help maintain a healthy lifestyle

Science: To develop hands-on inquiry, questioning, problem-solving, and hypothesizing skills and learn major science concepts and themes

Visual and performing arts: To expand communication and expression through art, music, dancing, drama, and aesthetics

Activities one through four on the following pages provide examples of ways in which SAC activities can integrate several curriculum and developmental areas while effectively involving a range of age groups.

Activity One
Sports Cards Collections

A favorite activity of many school-age children is collecting, talking about, and trading baseball and football cards. (Some children are also interested in collecting and trading other kinds of cards, such as those based on children's movies or stories.) The activity is popular because it can be undertaken without spending a great deal of money. Part of its attraction is also that it is an activity in which many adults and older children participate. Many programs have capitalized on this interest by establishing "card days" on which children may bring their cards to the center, look at others' collections, talk about the players and their records, and negotiate card trades with each other. The activity can remain informal or it can be structured by having the children create the guidelines.

Additional Learning Activities

- Play batting lineup. Each child on a team chooses his or her favorite player's card, then races with a person from another team to put the players in order of their batting record (or any other statistic you choose).

- Make "Be a star" cards. Each child chooses his or her desired or strongest area of accomplishment (sports, music, academics) and makes a card that features himself or herself as a performer. The children may draw their picture (or use a posed photograph) on the front of the card and write their statistics on the back.

- Read the sports page in the newspaper. Children read about their favorite sports players, then write stories using words they cut out of the sports section (e.g., "If I were *a famous athlete . . .*").

What the Activity Accomplishes

The sports cards can be used in different ways to emphasize skills and concepts in various age groups and curriculum and developmental areas and provide a lot of fun.

Age Group

Younger children: Classify numbers and place in order; receive cross-age assistance from older children who are team members.

Older children: Use multiplication and division skills to arrive at statistics; learn social compromise in negotiations; validate and share collections.

Oldest children: Use percentages in statistics; reinforce positive self-image; develop team leadership skills.

Developmental Area

Cognitive: Use mathematic skill; evaluate relative values.

Social–emotional: Interact in negotiations and teamwork; identify strengths and validate skills.

Curriculum Area

English–language arts: Talk about the cards and read the statistics.

Mathematics: Compare, order, and manipulate statistics; negotiate card values; use calculations to arrive at statistics.

History–social science: Identify and reinforce strengths; build self-esteem and self-knowledge.

Activity Two
Group Papier-mâché Sculptures

A favorite activity in many centers and with children of all ages is to make large papier-mâché figures as a group project. The figures can be fantasy creatures or represent a specific character or animal. Sometimes children choose to illustrate stories they have read or make the figures as props for a larger project, such as putting on a play or making a dinosaur. Whatever the purpose, the activity can engage all the children in many ways while they discuss, design, fabricate, and decorate their creation. This project is usually a long-term activity, and a place must be created in which work in progress can be left to dry and materials can be stored. In programs that share space, the activity may be a vacation program project enjoyed by all.

Additional Learning Activities

- Learn about the history of papier-mâché art in many cultures.
- Develop a diorama (like a museum exhibit) which includes papier-mâché figures. Use artwork or natural objects for the background and props to make the figures look as though they are in their natural surroundings.
- Experiment with various combinations of paper (e.g., newspaper and paper towels) and glue (e.g., starch, wallpaper paste, or combinations) to see which creates the best strength and texture.

What the Activity Accomplishes

This activity uses many different skills and levels of ability, enabling children at all developmental levels to have fun and be successful.

Age Group

Younger children: Participate in creative discussions with older children; work as part of the construction process; watch experiments with materials.

Older children: Participate in experiments; design characters or depict characters from stories.

Oldest children: Lead the engineering process; assist younger team members; design and carry out experiments; research the subject of the diorama.

Developmental Area

Cognitive: Develop workable designs and techniques; learn to plan ahead to develop a satisfactory product.

Social–emotional: Establish teamwork among different age groups and work styles to accomplish the project.

Linguistic: Initiate conversations and follow directions as the work progresses.

Physical: Develop small-muscle coordination in construction of figures (cutting, measuring, pasting, molding, and painting).

Creative: Design or invent a diorama.

Curriculum Area

English–language arts: Identify and develop character traits.

History–social science: Learn the history of other cultures that use the same materials and art medium.

Mathematics: Enlarge designs; estimate materials.

Science: Experiment with strength and texture of materials; research habitats; design structural strength of objects created.

Visual and performing arts: Work with a new art medium.

Activity Three
Group Performance

Children naturally love to perform, whether in a play, a fashion show, a lip-sync show, or an aerobics exhibition. SAC programs can provide the time, space, and freedom for children to design their own theme, choose the music, create costumes and props, and practice. The teachers may help children find appropriate materials and give suggestions on ways to accomplish their goals (as well as intervene in conflicts when needed), but the major work of developing the idea and making it work can and should be handled by the children.

Additional Learning Activities

- Put on a performance for parents, the children's school, or groups in the community.
- Make a videotape of the performance for later viewing or use on a local cable channel.
- Invite local performance groups to visit, share ideas, and put on their own performance.

What the Activity Accomplishes

Whatever kind of performance is selected, there is usually some way for every child to participate.

Age Group

Younger children: Perform roles; assist in making props; help with seating at performances.

Older children: Perform; make props and costumes; assist performers; make scenery; help with publicity.

Oldest children: Write scripts; stage the show; design costumes and props; assist and motivate younger children.

Developmental Area

Cognitive: Write the script or outline; develop a workable plan and time schedule; organize materials needed.

Linguistic: Develop public-speaking skills through performing.

Social–emotional: Develop leadership and teamwork skills to accomplish the project; feel satisfaction and self-esteem in performing successfully.

Creative: Use imagination in all areas of the production: scriptwriting, staging, acting, and performing.

Curriculum Area

English–language arts: Write a script or an outline of the performance.

Mathematics: Measure and enlarge drawings for scenery and props; time each segment of the performance and practice schedule.

Visual and performing arts: Identify, practice, and perform a skill or role; create the scenery and props; write musical scores; play instruments.

Activity Four

3-2-1, Contact Action Kit: Sports Theme (Science)

The Children's Television Workshop's curriculum materials for science were designed to help children in SAC programs learn about science in a fun, recreational, and active manner. For example, the 3-2-1 Contact Action Kit holds activity cards and videotapes entitled Sports, Detectives, Space, Stuff, and Architecture designed around particular science themes. Each activity deals with a science concept, but some of the cards can be used in other subject matter areas as well. You can use the cards to integrate science with other topics related to the particular theme, such as sports, or you may invent new activities, depending on the interests of the children.

Additional Learning Activities

- Use children's baseball or football cards to promote various mathematical activities.
- Hold a science fair based on a sports theme or organize a sports decathlon or sports festival.
- Create a sports videotape.
- Assess children's physical development and abilities and record their growth in particular sports or activities during the year. The observations and records can be shared with the children, or they might keep a record of their growth themselves.
- Help children with special needs learn to swing a bat or throw a ball by analyzing the task, breaking it down to its simplest steps, determining the child's skills, and adapting the activity.

What the Activity Accomplishes

Although the activity cards are designed for school-age children (five through twelve years old), some of the games are easier than others and can be played by the younger children, and some may be played by all the children or by the older ones, in particular. For example, the "Me" sports activity cards may be used by children of various ages for simple or more complex activities.

Age Group

Younger children: Read (with help from the teacher or older children) a "Me" sports activity card, which has instructions for children to make their own "Me" card (see Curriculum Area below); draw a picture of themselves and three sports they like to play. Some children might write the information, too.

Older children: Read the "Me" sports activity card and draw their own picture, indicating their height and weight; write three sports they like to play and three other things they like to do.

Oldest children: Design their own "Me" sports activity card and list on the back any teams they play on; make a "Me" card of themselves in five years, draw what they will look like, and name the sports they will play.

Curriculum Area

English–language arts (and science): "Me Card"—The card directs children to make sports cards about themselves, giving their physical descriptions and identifying things they like to do and teams on which they play.

Health (and science): "Body Builder"—The activity helps children find out which foods, particularly protein foods, make muscles strong. The children play a matching game based on linking proteins to the muscles they strengthen.

Physical education (and science): "Sports Charade"—Two teams develop synchronized movements and take turns to guess the other team's sport. "Signals: See What It Takes to Score"— Children learn different baseball signals, then play a simulated baseball board game.

Science: "Joint Adventure: Discover How Your Bones Come Together"—The directions read: "The only places your body can bend are at the joints. Choose one player to call out certain joints. When he [or she] says 'ball and sockets,' move those joints."

Social science (and science): "Face It: Muscle Up and Show Some Feelings"—The children learn about the muscles in their faces and detect what feeling they show when they move those muscles. They guess the particular muscles and feelings shown by others and discuss them.

Visual and performing arts (and science): "Shape Up, See Your Body Shape"—The card reads: "Different sports need different body shapes; find out about your body shape." The children trace each other's body shapes on a large piece of paper and color them.

Long-term Projects or Themes

Young children naturally develop theories to help them make sense of the world and learn about it, and they do that best through play. One way for older school-age children to learn naturally is through apprenticeships. One of the most important elements of apprenticeship is that it involves learning in a real-life context. A *cognitive apprenticeship* is a teaching strategy in which children come to understand the work of experts in a particular field as they work together on a project (Gardner 1993). Because children's work is their play and their play is also their work, the children will have fun while they are engaged in real-life work situations in the program. SAC staff could provide the children with such apprenticeship opportunities as establishing a store to sell items and raise funds, working on a SAC newspaper, or collecting grocery-store coupons to buy snacks for the program.

One way to create authentic work settings in a SAC program is through long-term projects related to a particular theme (Gardner 1993; Katz 1989). In a well-designed project the children engage in investigation using a variety of strategies and materials to solve problems and see relationships. The project can evolve out of the children's interests or hobbies. For example, one child's interest in camping might lead to a class project to learn about camping, with a camp trip planned for the end of the project. Projects might take place over an extended period of time, such as a week or a month. The length of time and complexity of the project and products would depend on the age of the children. Younger children are more involved in the immediate activities, but older children can remain involved over a longer period and are interested in a realistic product. Activities five and six present examples of long-term projects.

Long-term projects help children to integrate knowledge by using various intelligences and skills. The children can develop cognitively, socially, emotionally, physically, ethically, and creatively at the same time. Such projects involve cooperative work among the children in small and large groups, but children may choose to do individual projects, such as artwork. The children's contributions may differ, depending on their intellectual strengths or interests and the different ways children learn. By working together on long-term projects, children gain knowledge, develop socially, build self-esteem and feelings of success, and gain a positive attitude about learning (Katz 1989). The completed work, such as a play or festival, can be presented before an audience.

Pen Pals Project

Some of the children in the group may want to have penpals who live elsewhere. The pen pals may live in other towns or out-of-state or even in other countries. There may be a number of reasons for wanting to write to someone who lives somewhere else. Some of the children in your program may come from different towns, states, or regions of the United States or from other countries. If so, they may still have friends or relatives in those places and wish to select pen pals from those areas, or a group of children might write to one person from another area.

Additional Learning Activities

- Mail overseas letters and packages at the post office; decide what to put in the letters and packages; determine mailing costs.
- Take pictures of SAC children to include in the letters and packages.
- Read books and stories and listen to music from the region or country in which the pen pal lives.
- Look at globes and maps to see where the pen pal's country is located.
- Write letters to other kinds of pen pals, such as grandparents or other relatives.
- Invite parents or people from the community, especially if they are from another country or place, to talk about their cultural values and customs.
- Cook a meal and make a recipe book, using some of the recipes of the country discussed.

What the Activity Accomplishes

Children have the opportunity to learn how children in other areas live and what they think about and play. The project gives children a chance to communicate with other children over a long period of time and establish a long-term friendship.

Age Group

Younger children: Write a group letter, which they can dictate to a staff member who writes it down in front of them; understand how letters are written and what a letter-writing format looks like; learn how to address an envelope; communicate with other children through the written word.

Older children: Write their own letters; check their spelling; talk about themselves and what they like to do; find out what children in other areas like to do, eat, and play; make a friend through written communication; develop a long-term friendship.

Oldest children: Write their own letter to a child or adult pen pal; determine whom they should select as a pen pal and why; analyze their letter for content and think about how it would sound to someone who lives somewhere else; help younger children write a group or short individual letter; help translate letters into another language, if necessary.

Curriculum Area

English–language arts: Write letters; read books.

History–social science: Read about the history of the country the child comes from; analyze reasons for any economic problems; discuss how people make a living in that country compared with people in your community; learn about other cultures, customs, and geographic areas; learn how a post office works; become more empathetic to and appreciative of the experiences of people from other cultures.

Mathematics: Count money for post office stamps and packages; weigh and measure packages before sending them to find out how much will fit in the packages.

Physical education: Play games and sports popular in other places.

Visual and performing arts: Dance, sing, and listen to music of other countries, regions, and cultures. Invent songs that combine the rhythms, instruments, and lyrics of other countries with the music found in the children's own culture. Make folk costumes or study the artwork of other cultures. Incorporate these into your art projects.

Activity Six
Homeless Project

Some of the children in the program may have gone to the shopping mall or the downtown area in their community and noticed the number of homeless children and their families walking around or asking for money or food. The SAC children may have asked their parents about those families and wondered why some of the people are dirty or do not have shoes or warm coats. The parents may have said that the families are homeless. The children may wonder why those families are homeless and raise the question in a class discussion in the SAC program.

In the group talk about the reasons children might be homeless: parents who are unemployed; a family which has moved from another area and the parent or parents cannot find work; or a parent who is disabled or has an emotional or health problem or addiction. Talk about what it means to be homeless, why the children are not in school, and what the residency laws are. Some of the younger children in the program may be afraid of the homeless children and their families and say, "They're dirty! Yuk!" Some of the older children may look down on those families and say, "Why don't they get a job? What's wrong with them?"

Children need help to understand the issues of homelessness and to empathize with and, perhaps, take some action to assist the families. The staff may use role-playing as a way to help the children "step into the shoes" of homeless children and empathize with them by learning what is happening to them. That may lead to a desire by the children to help out in some way.

Additional Learning Activities

- Role-play some incidents or problems that involve homeless families; suggest the children step into the shoes of a homeless child to see how he or she feels.

- Establish a SAC buddy program to assist and connect with a homeless family or child. Decide what the child needs, such as a school backpack, pencils, a lock for school lockers, or other materials, to help the child in school once he or she is enrolled. Plan a fund-raising project to raise the money for this activity.

What the Activity Accomplishes

The project helps children begin to develop empathy for others and, perhaps, take some sort of action to assist people.

Age Group

Younger children: Talk about how they would feel if they had to go to bed hungry or if they did not have shoes, a hat, or gloves to wear in the wintertime. Talk about how they would feel if they were cold at night or did not have their own bed in which to sleep. Become involved in socio-dramatic play in which they become a homeless child; talk about how they felt.

Older children: Discuss in a small group how it might feel to stand on a corner with a sign asking for food. Role-play some stories of unfinished problems that involve homeless families, act out the different roles, then talk about how they felt. Talk about how to solve the unfinished problem; explore different ways of solving the problem.

Oldest children: Discuss what has caused the rise in the homeless problem and what the children can do at their level to reduce the problem. Plan a fund-raiser and carry it out. Research how money can be used in a helpful, socially sensitive way that does not offend anyone.

Curriculum Area

Health: Help collect canned goods for homeless families; discuss health needs of the families.

History–social science: Discuss needs of homeless families; learn to empathize with and become sensitive to the social and economic plights of people; reduce stereotypic and discriminatory attitudes; learn to help solve social problems by taking a stand or doing something positive.

Mathematics: Read statistics about homeless people in that area; determine funds needed to purchase materials or to send a check; count money raised before making purchases.

Use of Several Skills and Concepts

Many SAC activities do an excellent job of bringing together and integrating several different skills and concepts in one fun activity. The following are examples of such activities.

Fun Activities
Using Several Skills and Concepts

1. *English–language arts + art*

   Making flannel-board stories to share with younger children

   Children read stories and choose their favorite to rewrite in their own script, illustrate, and create in flannel-board pieces so that they can present the story to younger children. The older children learn how to tell a story in their own words while they focus on characters, place setting, and action or plot points. The activity builds the self-esteem of older children because of the work they do with younger children.

2. *Mathematics + music + science*

   Making acoustic instruments

   Children learn about the science of acoustics (sound) while they experiment with materials and shapes and use mathematical planning skills to measure and cut pieces for their instruments. The children come to understand musical pitch and notation as they learn to play the instrument and write down their compositions.

3. *Science + art + mathematics*

   Making tie-dyed art and modeling dough from a recipe

   These fun activities involve children in measurement, computation, and ratios. As the children follow and enlarge recipes for the dye and the modeling dough, they see also how various substances interact with each other. Children use their mixtures in creative ways and experiment with various combinations of color, texture, and pattern.

Curriculum-based Skills and Concepts

The following in-depth activities are designed to enhance some of the elementary-school skills and concepts described in the curriculum frameworks.

1. *English–language arts.* The goals are to develop and integrate listening, speaking, reading, writing, and language skills and an appreciation of literature through a language arts, writing, reading, and phonics program.

Putting on a puppet show

Children plan, write, and put on a puppet show for other children in the program.

Skills and concepts utilized: Writing an original story or adapting an existing story into dialogue style requires thinking about how people speak to each other, writing down one's thoughts, and editing and refining the script. Children practice critical-thinking, problem-solving, discussion, and communication skills as teams work together to design and create the characters of the puppets for the show. Performers are involved in reading the script as they perform their parts as narrators or puppeteers. Children who view the show practice listening skills, which may be enhanced when the children are asked to suggest possible new endings for the story.

2. *Health.* The goals are to accept responsibility for one's personal health; respect and promote the health of others; understand the process of growth and development; and acquire health-related information and knowledge of health products and services.

Preparing for emergencies

Children work with staff to update emergency procedures, learn simple first-aid techniques, and ensure that appropriate emergency supplies are in an easily accessible place. Staff and children then dramatize an emergency, such as an earthquake, and act out the steps they would take in the emergency.

Skills and concepts utilized: Children prepare for emergencies and learn how to recognize such situations; learn how to use basic first-aid procedures and how to obtain help when necessary; learn the stop-drop-and-roll technique to use in the event of a fire; and practice appropriate behavior in disaster drills.

Promoting a healthy SAC program

Children, particularly the older ones, investigate ways in which their SAC program promotes health and make recommendations for changes that staff might make to further encourage health at the site. For example, children critically examine the food choices offered; their access to hand-washing facilities; their opportunities to participate in a variety of enjoyable physical activities; the center's handling of children who become ill while in the center; and staff–child interactions and child-to-child interactions to determine whether those interactions promote a sense of belonging and foster resiliency. Children may break into teams to do their research and evaluation of the program, then share their results with the whole group.

Skills and concepts utilized: Children make healthy food choices; promote good personal hygiene; participate in a variety of enjoyable physical activities; demonstrate care and compassion toward people who are ill and take steps to ensure that others stay healthy; demonstrate good communication and friendship skills; develop and maintain a positive outlook; and appreciate differences and similarities among children and staff.

3. *History–social science.* The goals are to develop social participation skills, critical-thinking skills, cultural knowledge and understanding, democratic and civic values, and knowledge of history and social science disciplines.

Creating a country

Children create their own country, giving it a name and describing the flag, language, housing, national song, food, costumes, ways of making and spending money, and type of government.

Skills and concepts utilized: Children learn about cultural attributes, such as what kinds of things differ from culture to culture and what tends to stay the same; economics and the use of money; and types of government, such as democratic, dictatorial, or parliamentary.

Forming a court of appeals

Children form their own court system to help settle disputes between children. Some children become the attorneys, members of the jury, or the judge and discuss what their roles and responsibilities are. The children may use such props as the U.S. flag, a judge's gavel, and judge's robe to carry out the courtroom drama.

Skills and concepts utilized: Children come to understand the workings of the judicial system and develop listening, critical-thinking, and decision-making skills and civic values.

4. *Mathematics.* The goals are to learn numbers, measurement,

geometry, logic, algebra, estimation, mental arithmetic, probability, statistics, pattern and function relationships, variables and operations, problem-solving and computational skills, and the use of computers and calculators.

Planning a summer field-trip lunch

Children assist in planning the supplies and equipment needed to create a picnic or barbecue at the beach.

Skills and concepts utilized: Children estimate how much they think they will need; count the number of people going and how many sandwiches they will eat; compute the number of slices of bread, slices of cheese, and so forth they will need (for example, for 75 kids and six adults to have two sandwiches each); and calculate how much that will cost, based on advertisements and use of coupons from local grocery stores.

Challenging consumer brands

Children stage their own challenges by selecting popular items, such as corn chips and salsa, based on preferences related to taste or to the amount of fat, salt, or sugar in those items.

Skills and concepts utilized: Children hypothesize and estimate, making a chart of initial guesses about the percentage of children preferring each brand; perform statistics by taking a poll of children to indicate each one's preference and charting the results by percentage in bar graphs and pie charts; and engage in experimental methodology by setting up and running a blind taste test between brands to determine actual preferences and charting the results.

5. *Physical education.* The goals are to develop movement, personal, and social skills that promote physical activity and a healthy lifestyle.

Learning aerobic dancing

School-age children enjoy learning the steps and routines associated with aerobic dancing through videotaped routines. Staff who take aerobics or staff from local dance or exercise studios may volunteer to teach aerobic dancing at the center for a few hours each week. To enhance children's interest, plan a performance for parents and other children in which participants use the learned routines along with costumes and props made in conjunction with art or sewing projects.

Skills and concepts utilized: Children acquire knowledge of certain dance steps, develop skills and grace in movement, become physically fit, maintain wellness, and improve their self-image.

Children work in teams to create life-sized tracings of themselves. The children lie down on double sheets of butcher paper that are longer than they are, and their partners trace around their bodies with pencils. The children then fill in their features as accurately as possible and draw in their hair, eyes, and skin color, using mirrors to duplicate their personal "color palette." The program needs to provide sets of paints or crayons in a wide range of colors.

When the drawing is complete, cut along the traced outline of both layers of the paper, stuff the area between the two layers with crumpled newspaper, and staple the edges to create a three-dimensional figure. These figures may be dressed in the children's own clothes or decorated before cutting to represent a desired outfit or an appropriate ethnic costume. The children can talk about the similarities and differences among themselves and discuss what causes the differences. The "me" figures may be displayed around the room for parents to see.

Skills and concepts utilized: Children develop a sense of their physical selves, including their height, length of arms and legs, proportion, body type (muscular, lean, etc.), skin color, and hair color; learn about the muscular structure and parts of the body; understand what causes physical differences among people and groups; and develop a positive physical self-image.

6. *Science.* The goals are to learn the scientific processes of hands-on inquiry, questioning, problem solving, and hypothesizing and some of the major scientific theories for linking facts and ideas, such as energy, patterns of change, stability, and systems and interactions.

Making water markers

Children make markers to draw on the sidewalks by freezing water in containers that can be peeled away, such as paper straws or frozen-juice containers.

Skills and concepts utilized: Children observe the change in form from liquid to solid as ice develops; from solid to liquid as the ice melts in drawing on the sidewalk; and from liquid to gas as the water evaporates and disappears. Discuss the transformations and ask the children to hypothesize while they proceed through each step of the activity about what will happen next and why they think that process happens.

Making a volcano in the sandbox

Build a central core for the volcano out of two or three empty frozen-juice cans taped together end to end, then build a volcanic mountain around the core with wet sand. Create a "lava" flow by pouring red tempera (paint), baking soda, and vinegar into the bottom of the core. Children can expand their knowledge of volcanic action by building a village around the base of the volcano and watching what happens to it when the lava mixture flows out.

Skills and concepts utilized: Children analyze what happened in the experiment involving earth science (volcanic activity), chemistry (chemical reaction of baking soda and vinegar), problem solving (discovery of the optimum amounts of baking soda, vinegar, and tempera to create the best lava flow), and hypothesizing (tentative explanation of volcanic eruption).

7. *Visual and performing arts.* The goals are to expand avenues of communication and self-expression; enjoy aesthetic expression by appreciating originality in creative works; develop skills in arts and crafts; and learn to use the arts as an expression of feelings.

Making prints

In an introduction to print making, many different types of prints can be exhibited. Artistic works, such as early woodcut drawings, primitive woodcuts from various cultures, complex lithographs, and silk screens, should be displayed for children to examine and appreciate. Children can learn from the displays and create prints from simple materials when taught basic skills. They may experiment with more complex and advanced techniques as their interests and abilities dictate. Docents from local museums or college art programs and local artisans can be invited to share ideas.

Skills and concepts utilized: Children develop print-making skills; understand the history of the print-making process; and learn to appreciate prints from many cultures.

Dancing

Begin with the dance forms in which children express an interest, whether their interest lies in current street-dancing movements or classical ballet steps. Present various styles of dance for children to try. For example, older children can teach younger children steps that they have learned; local high school or college students may volunteer to teach a particular dance; and teachers from local studios or theater groups may volunteer their services. Each child may watch or participate as he or she chooses. A social dance or performance at the end of the series of dance workshops will offer an added incentive to become involved.

Skills and concepts utilized: Children learn various forms and styles of dance; explore their senses through movement; develop the art of composing dances (choreography); and become comfortable with different types of dance, such as ballet, tap, jazz, modern, or ethnic.

Making a musical videotape

Children make their own musical videotape; different children carry out various responsibilities in producing the videotape. The children share their creation with other groups and with their parents.

Skills and concepts utilized: Children write lyrics to be memorized; write the action plan for the videotape; and outline and schedule the production. Teams plan, negotiate, and decide together how to communicate their message to the audience. Children listen to original music carefully and write down lyrics to be memorized. Children who view the tape watch and listen closely to the finished product to see how their friends perform.

Varying the Activities

Even the most balanced program of activities can become boring when the same activities are offered repeatedly. Although you must be sure to include all the important developmental and other elements in your program, you need also to vary the way in which you present those elements to the children. If your program includes a magazine-collage art project every Thursday, that creative opportunity probably will not achieve its purpose because children will stop participating in the activity. By varying the presentation of activities, you can keep the children interested and happily engaged.

Although adults plan and present many activities in the program, activities may also take shape in the minds of the children, who may enjoy planning their own project. Given adult permission and encouragement, children can develop many wonderful ideas that will both enrich the program and allow the children to feel a sense of involvement and pride in the program. However, for a project to be truly a child-initiated project, children's participation must be voluntary. Requiring children to participate in a project today that they excitedly planned yesterday takes the activity from the realm of child-initiated to staff-initiated. In planning child-initiated activities, keep in mind that children at earlier developmental stages have less need to create their own activities; they may even become frustrated and confused when faced with too many choices and too little structure.

One element of activities that you can easily change to create new excitement and creative thought is the type or variety of media you provide. Art projects are much more fun when you have lots of colors and textures from which to choose as you try to create the picture you have in mind. Sculpturing and woodworking take on new excitement when new materials are introduced. Creating this kind of variety does not necessarily require a large budget. Some parents may work for companies that discard interesting paper or materials used in a manufacturing process. Local businesses are often cooperative about saving and donating scrap materials to SAC programs. Be resourceful and be willing to ask.

Children, like adults, often get tired of seeing the same buildings and furniture day after day. One way to provide some variety for children is to arrange occasional off-site activities using resources available in the community. Have the staff brainstorm or research places within walking distance of the program that the children might visit. Local businesses (especially those whose employees have children in your program) will often be willing to arrange for a tour of their operation. Because one of the main problems for many businesses is lack of space, you may have to offer the experience to small groups—although business people may be surprisingly receptive to visits by children. Other trips into the community might include walking (or riding public transportation) to a local store to buy supplies or visiting the local library.

In addition to the people who are willing to let you visit them, there are people who will be happy to visit you. For example, local police and fire departments and institutions, such as zoos and museums, are often cooperative about sending representatives to programs for children. If you have a college in your community, you may find students or teachers willing to share their interests and expertise in such areas as children's theater or science for an afternoon. Local hobby organizations may have people who will come and share their interest in quilting, stamp collecting, or building aviation models. Brainstorm possibilities in a staff meeting and assign people to contact suitable speakers. However, make sure that you discuss with the guest beforehand what he or she will talk about and for how long. Do not hesitate to tell people how long children will realistically sit and listen and the kinds of things that interest children.

An important feature of SAC programs is the wide range of ages served concurrently. To meet the needs of all children in your program, you must design activities that raise challenges for the older children but do not exclude the younger ones from success. Projects in which a variety of roles must be filled are ideal for SAC programs; children can take on jobs with which they feel comfortable and still be part of the final result. Games with variable rules also work well. Children at earlier stages of development may receive advantages (such as batting from a T-ball stand or being allowed extra strikes) while older children are challenged by more demanding rules. Activities with no defined product (such as paper or clay sculpture) lend themselves well to mixed age groups because children create their own ideas of success.

One way to categorize projects is by the kind of result accomplished. Older children tend to be more concerned about a tangible, realistic product, and younger children are more excited about the process involved in creation. In some projects children produce such items as pictures or vases that each child can take home either the same day or on completion of a longer project. In other projects children create consumable items for participants to share, such as a pizza or soup. Another possibility is for children to combine their efforts in a large group project, such as making a clubhouse or quilt to be shared at the center. Some group projects, such as putting on a play or musical performance, produce nothing tangible or lasting except in memory. When you plan your activities, it is important to balance projects based on the kind of result that children achieve. All children will eventually get tired of making things that cannot be taken home, but cooperative projects that produce shared results are beneficial and should not be ignored.

Although children in SAC programs need many varied activities so that they do not get bored, they also need some time or space to do nothing or to be alone. During outdoor playtime some children may want to sit by themselves and simply think or daydream. Young children, in particular, tire easily and may become cranky if overstimulated. Staff need to plan for varying intensity levels in the program so that there is a balance between slow and fast, loud and soft, active and quiet, and creative and structured activities.

Using Different Methods of Presentation

To meet the needs of the varied ages, personalities, backgrounds, preferences, and special needs of children in SAC programs, it is important to use many different methods of presenting activities. Methods that work well in SAC programs are shown on the following page.

Experiment with the different methods and find the balance that works with your children. Be sure to consider whether children from different cultural backgrounds are more or less comfortable with certain kinds of activities; for example, whether they prefer noncompetitive or competitive activities. Find out about the children's preferences from the parents and adjust your presentation methods accordingly. All suggestions can be adapted for children with special needs by taking into account their interests and abilities.

All children and adults have a natural learning preference that determines how they absorb information most effectively. When you must explain rules, techniques, or skills for activities, present the information in a manner that will address each child's learning style:

- *Auditory learners* learn best through what they hear. Use explanations, discussions, questions, and answers.
- *Visual learners* learn best through what they see. Use demonstrations, charts, and hand and body gestures.
- *Kinesthetic learners* learn best through physical involvement. Use the children as models in short practice sessions.

Recent studies have determined that intellectual functioning is composed of many different types of intelligence (discussed previously in the section "How Children Grow and Develop"). Children have different strengths in different areas of intelligence and tend to use their areas of strength more than they use other functions that may be weaker. See Table 6 for the seven types of intelligence that have been identified and some of the activities that exercise each intelligence.

In balancing activities, you need to ensure that all areas of intelligence are represented. You must not only provide children with successes in their strong areas but also encourage them to develop in areas that may be weaker. You may also help children to grow in certain intelligences by letting children start activities with the intelligence with which they are most comfortable and capable and, later, transferring the focus of the activity to make use of a less-developed intelligence. For example, a child might create an art project (spatial), then be asked to discuss that work (linguistic).

When integrating children with special needs into your program, keep in mind the philosophy that these children are

Presentation Methods

Learning centers	Small groups of children work together on directed tasks (e.g., a folder game that teaches mathematic skills).
Clubs or special-interest groups	Small groups of children with shared interests learn or use skills in a sequence of planned activities.
Child-initiated or child-designed activities	Children plan and carry out activities that emerge from their own ideas.
Games	Activities include competitive and noncompetitive formats.
Free play	Children choose activities from several areas and available equipment.
Discovery centers	Displays and collections of materials encourage individual or small-group exploration and experimentation.

children first. They have the same needs for success and acceptance as any child, and staff must be sensitive to the limitations of all children. Many children with special needs will be able to integrate into your program with very little adaptation, but you may need to vary your presentation methods. Successful program planning takes into account what the child can do and adds reasonable challenges and goals to activities.

Table 6

Seven Intelligences
and Related SAC Activities

Intelligence	Related Activity
Bodily/kinesthetic	Games requiring coordination, dancing, sports
Interpersonal	Projects, games, and activities involving cooperation and teamwork; class meetings and discussions to solve interpersonal problems, such as name calling
Intrapersonal	Self-esteem activities, writing of autobiographies, and "How I feel" activities
Linguistic	Word games, creative writing, discussions
Logical/mathematical	Number games, puzzles, mazes, science experiments, water play with different-sized containers
Musical	Activities that involve playing instruments, singing, listening to music
Spatial	Block construction, manipulative toys, three-dimensional art projects

To ensure that the activities you are encouraging children with disabilities to participate in are appropriate, take a few minutes to analyze what is needed to complete the activity. Compare the requirements of the activity with the abilities of the child. This assessment will give you a good indication of whether or not the activity is right for the child. Use the following steps to make that determination:

1. Analyze the activity and break it down to its simplest steps.
2. Assess the child's skills and concepts to determine whether he or she possesses the physical, social–emotional, and cognitive skills and concepts necessary to complete the activity. Ask the question: Can the child complete the steps described in the task analysis? If the answer is yes, go ahead and try the activity with the child. If the answer is no, determine what adaptations you can make that would enable the child to successfully participate in the activity.
3. If the child cannot successfully participate in the activity, even with adaptations, select an alternative activity, analyze the skills required, and start working on those skills with the child through simplified versions of the activity.

Children tend to react to demands and orders in much the same way that adults do, often by rebelling or refusing to cooperate. Teachers need to find ways to encourage children to participate in activities rather than force them to do so. Try to include the following techniques in planning and presenting activities:

- Plan activities based on what children say they want to do.

SAC programs must support children's self-esteem by providing successful experiences, surrounding them with adults who value them, and encouraging them to believe in themselves

- Be enthusiastic about the activity.
- Be flexible and change the activity as you go along, incorporating children's needs and ideas.
- Allow children to try the activity for ten minutes before they commit to playing.
- Partner enthusiastic children with more reluctant children.
- Ask less enthusiastic children to be helpers or group leaders.

When activities are presented effectively and children have choices, the children will be more involved and enthusiastic.

Enriching Children's Lives

One of the best things staff can do for children is to help them cope well with their lives outside the program. Children spend a lot of time at home and in school, and SAC programs can do many things to equip children to thrive in those environments. When planning activities, consider the following factors to foster well-rounded children.

Children will eventually move beyond your SAC program and will need to know how to care for themselves effectively. Staff can support children's growing need for independence and self-sufficiency by providing experiences in which the children can learn how to function in society. For example, children can have fun learning such crucial skills as how to use telephone directories, maps, and newspapers. Staff can encourage positive attitudes about exercise and nutrition, helping children to become healthy and fit. Children also need problem-solving and decision-making skills, which can be taught and reinforced in your program.

Children need to learn to make independent and positive choices about how they use their free time. Staff can help by exposing children to activities that can be pursued at the center as well as at home, such as getting involved in crafts or collections. Staff can also help children learn and enjoy games and sports that children may find are fun ways to spend their free time. Teachers may need to point out to children that an activity they enjoy at the center could also be done at home, then help them figure out how materials or teammates might be found.

Self-esteem springs from a feeling of personal value and trust in one's skills and abilities. Children who think poorly of themselves and believe that feeling is shared by others are far less likely to be successful and happy adults than children who believe in themselves. Children do not enter life with high or low self-esteem. The people around them send a lot of messages about their worth and desirability, and those messages translate into internal voices that support or undermine children's motivation. SAC programs must support children's self-esteem by providing successful experiences, surrounding them with adults who value them, and encouraging them to believe in themselves. SAC staff must genuinely like to work with and believe in school-age children because those feelings are transmitted to the children.

A crucial part of life for school-age children is having friends. However, the skills that allow children to interact appropriately with others do not just appear. Those skills are learned and fostered throughout childhood. SAC programs need to create ways for children to work in groups, allow children to "hang out" and interact on their own, and help children identify and practice the social skills that will allow them to enter groups and get along with people successfully. Some of the most important social skills children can learn are conflict resolution and mutual prob-

lem solving. No one is immune to occasional conflicts with others, but if people know some ways to solve interpersonal problems so that everyone gets some of what he or she needs, conflicts will be less likely to escalate to major fights and wars.

Children today live their lives in a diverse world. They are surrounded by people who may be like or unlike themselves in culture, language, customs, ability, and appearance. To be professionally and personally successful, children must develop an acceptance, understanding, and appreciation of diverse traits. Children are not born with either a positive or negative view of others. They are taught by their parents, their teachers, the media, and their peers what constitutes an "okay" person. Although the opinions of those other groups may differ, staff must try to help children see that people are more alike than different and that different is not bad, just different.

Another important life skill is the ability to look at things from a new angle, beyond the way they appear to be. Children need to learn to think for themselves, evaluate information and ideas, and form their own conclusions. Creative thinking springs from the ability to look beyond the obvious to see the possible. Progress comes from people who have developed that skill. Young adults who learn to think critically and creatively will have a major advantage in life. SAC programs can support that skill by encouraging children to figure things out and solve their own problems as much as possible and by creating experiences in which answers are not obvious.

Chapter 4

Creating SAC Environments

The environment in your SAC center is an important part of the program you provide and includes far more than just the way you arrange the furniture and hang the pictures on the wall. The organization and care of the physical facility, including indoor and outdoor space, and the emotional environment of the program send powerful messages to the children and their families. The physical and emotional environments are critical factors in the flow of the program, the children's moods, and the kinds of activities and choices that are offered. The physical layout and furnishings should add to the growth and development of children at various ages and levels of interest and need.

Sending Messages Through the Environment

The way in which you use and arrange your facility is a big part of the message you send to children about themselves and their place in your program. The following are some important messages for children and suggestions on how to send those messages through your environment:

1. *You are welcome here.*
   - Display the children's work and projects prominently and attractively and treat the work as valuable items.
   - Provide a safe place for each child's personal belongings.
   - Reflect a wide variety of ethnic, cultural, and economic backgrounds in displays and in program materials, such as books and records; pay particular attention to the cultures and languages of the families participating in the center. Select nonstereotypical, culturally responsive materials that present ethnic groups in a positive, capable, authentic light.
   - Display notes and information for parents in an attractive manner near the entrance to the program.
   - Ensure that space and materials are adaptable for children with special needs and differing abilities.

2. *This is a safe place.*
   - Keep furniture and equipment clean and well maintained.
   - Post rules reflecting the need for kindness and cooperation in conspicuous areas and enforce the rules.
   - Establish protected areas in which children can be alone and quiet when they wish to be.

3. *We trust your ability to make good choices and be independent.*
   - Display activity choices and schedules for children to see.
   - Organize and store materials in a way that enables children to select items and put them away independently.

4. *You can have fun here.*
   - Provide areas and equipment for many different kinds of play and exploration activities.
   - Rotate toys and games to provide new interests and challenges.
   - Display results of past projects and activities.

Arranging the Environment to Meet Program Purposes

It is important for children to have the opportunity to participate in different kinds of activities after school, depending on their needs and interests. Arrange the environment to meet children's needs as indicated:

1. Group size and level of isolation
   - Places to be alone—a quiet reading corner or a shady tree
   - Places to play with a few friends—small game tables or an enclosed dramatic-play area
   - Places to play in large groups—a kickball field or "balloon volleyball" court
2. Ability level
   - Places in which parallel activities requiring different skill levels can take place—a woodworking center with various projects using different tools and techniques
   - Places which can accommodate the same kind of activity at various skill or interest levels—a reading or music area offering a variety of books, magazines, records, or tape-recorded stories
3. Energy level
   - Places for quiet or low-key activities—a conversation corner, a table for playing with manipulative toys, or learning centers for one or two children
   - Places to be moderately active—a dramatic-play area for pretend games or an art area for messy projects
   - Places for high-energy play—a "four-square" court or "Frisbee-golf" course

Developmentally Appropriate Activities

You need to establish an environment in which children are able to engage in developmentally appropriate activities. *Developmentally appropriate* means that the activities, materials, and equipment provided to the children suit their particular age group and individual and cultural needs. It means the activities are meaningful to the children, fit their backgrounds, experiences, and values, and have been adapted to any special needs the children may have. It means the activities are neither too advanced nor too simple, but children learn while having fun and by being actively involved. The following are examples of activities that relate to children's developmental needs and the SAC environments that encourage those activities:

Children learn while having fun and by being actively involved.

- *Making choices.* Make available simultaneously many activities and materials from which children can choose, such as an art area, a reading or quiet conversation area, an outdoor games area, a homework area, and a games table area.
- *Taking responsibility.* Arrange and label storage areas and containers so that children can clean up after their own activities and become involved in the maintenance of their program materials. Use see-through plastic boxes to store manipulative toys so that children know where each toy belongs.
- *Using imagination.* Provide spaces and furnishings that can be used in many ways and that can be adapted to the activities developed by the children. Examples of multiuse materials are plastic crates, which can become seats in a pretend house or school, parts of an obstacle course, "holes" in Frisbee golf, or a means for transporting materials for outdoor art projects. Include special equipment, such as large-print books, or adapted playground equipment, such as wheelchair-accessible structures, depending on the children's disabilities, so that all children can be creative.
- *Exploring a variety of interests.* Regularly change the content of activity centers and the selection of equipment and materials available to the children. For example, a "discovery" area may contain different kinds of lenses (magnifiers, telescopes, old plastic prescription eyeglass lenses, or prisms) for a week; then the contents may be changed to include several old, small appliances (with the cords removed), such as hairdryers, clocks, or office machines, that can be taken apart and explored.

- *Creating a personal environment.* Provide materials and activities that fit the children's cultures, home values, or primary language. Provide opportunities for the children to share their values and experiences in a natural, integrative manner.

Children's Behavior

A consistent problem reported by SAC staff is dealing with the active and often challenging nature of school-age children's behavior. Encourage the kind of behavior you want from children by organizing your environment as follows:

1. Avoid space conflicts.
   - Place quiet activities away from high-energy play areas to avoid conflicts between children about noise and interruptions.
   - Conduct activities that involve sitting or lying on the floor in areas that are not part of the traffic patterns of your program.
   - Create safe spaces for children to play by arranging furniture so that it directs the flow of traffic around the play area.
2. Maintain program materials and equipment.
   - Encourage children to respect and care for materials, games, books, and toys by keeping supplies in good repair or removing articles from the program when damaged. Books that are ripped and written in send the message that it is OK to tear books or to write in them. Have children help fix the books or plan and carry out a project to raise money to purchase new books.
   - Place messy activities in an area with easy clean-up features, such as running water and hard floor surfaces. Mixing and playing with "sawdust dough" in the kitchen, outdoors, or on the tile floor (rather than over the carpet) will create less conflict between children and staff about making a mess.

Encourage the kind of behavior you want from children by organizing your environment

   - Involve children in the regular program cleanup and provide a transitional warning ("You will need to start cleaning up in five minutes") to allow children time to finish the activity before cleaning up the area or activity.
3. Use the size of the space to control behavior.
   - Provide the right amount of space for activities. Too much space can be distracting for small groups or quiet activities and may encourage running and loud voices, which are more appropriate outdoors.

Closing off certain areas with room dividers or covering unused equipment with sheets helps to control how space and equipment are used.

- Avoid conflicts and disruptions that tend to occur when children are cramped together in space which is too small for the group. If the snack area is too small and eight children must be seated at tables made for six, serve the snacks in shifts or individually as children arrive at the program after school.

Organizing Program Areas

Providing designated areas for different kinds of activities helps children identify their choices and the behaviors that are appropriate for each area. Organizing such areas also enables you to store supplies and equipment near the area in which they will be used so that they are readily accessible and do not have to be transported. The information in Table 7 will guide you in designating and designing activity areas within your program.

In addition to the children's activities, you need to consider other facets of program operation, such as those in Table 8, when designing an effective, functional environment.

An important element in the design of SAC program space is flexibility. A flexible design enables you to adapt the spaces to the changing needs and interests of the children and staff. The design should allow for the following factors:

Reflecting children's interests. The facility needs to accommodate the activities that children originate because of their interests. As children's interests change and their skills develop, there should be places for the children to try new activities and materials to stimulate their creativity.

Accommodating new staff or equipment. New staff bring special skills and interests that should be incorporated into the program. The facility may need to be redesigned to accommodate a new activity area or the purchase or donation of new equipment.

Extending school-day activities. Children's interests will also change as a result of activities and issues presented during the school day. Children benefit greatly from fun activities that reinforce skills learned or concepts taught in school. SAC programs also can provide opportunities for hands-on, extended projects that clarify learning for many children.

Ensuring "line-of-sight" supervision. When placing large pieces of furniture, ensure that the staff's ability to keep children in sight from all parts of the room is not impaired. Use low cabinets to create sheltered areas that staff can see into and, therefore, supervise.

Table 7
Activity Areas

Arts and Crafts	An area with tables and chairs on a hard floor near running water. Can include art supplies that are readily available to children; supplies and equipment for special, planned activities; and spaces for drying or storing children's work until completion.
Manipulative Toys	A sheltered, carpeted area in which manipulative toys, such as blocks or building bricks, are stored and in which children can sit on the floor or at small tables to construct creations.
Board Games and Puzzles	An area with tables and chairs and which has direct access to games, puzzles, and small manipulatives. Computers that involve games or programs for two children may be included here, too.
Music/Language Arts	An area in which quiet music may be played on tape recorders, record players, or compact disc players. Children may use headsets, combine headsets with the use of slide projectors or filmstrips, or write stories in this area.
Quiet Reading/Conversation	A well-lit sheltered area with soft places to sit, such as pillows, beanbag chairs, or sofas, and with direct access to a variety of reading materials.
Science and Discovery	An area with table and chairs that can be used to observe experiments and which has space for materials that children can explore; live plants and animals children may care for and observe; and bulletin boards to use for displays. May include science equipment, such as microscopes, batteries, and wire; materials for specific experiments or demonstrations; and collections, such as bottle caps, rocks, shells, stamps. Pose an open-ended science question each week for the students to solve and discuss the ways they arrived at answers.
Dramatic Play	An area with scaled furniture to create a pretend house or an open area with dress-up clothes, mirrors, and dramatic play kits, with props to create play offices, restaurants, schools, and shops. Include multicultural items, such as chopsticks, rice bowls, and empty cans of various types of ethnic food related to the culture of children in the program.
Homework	A quiet area with tables and chairs. Adequate lighting should be available as well as carpet squares or a small rug to define the work space. It is helpful for children to have direct access to school supplies, such as paper, pencils, calculators, abacuses, dictionaries, encyclopedias, and typewriters or computers.
Cooking	An area away from the main traffic patterns, preferably near running water and electrical outlets. This activity is usually not a permanent fixture except in programs which have a kitchen on the premises.
Large-group Play	A large open space, either indoors or outdoors (preferably both), in which large groups of children can participate in games, sports, dancing, or playing musical instruments.

Table 8
Other Program Areas

Parent Area

An area in which parents can sign children in and out of the program, leave and receive messages, and learn about program issues. The area may consist of a bulletin board with program notices and log sheets or be a comfortable area with a parent library, coffee, places for individual messages, and materials for parents to use to leave notes for staff.

Isolation Area

A comfortable place in which children who become ill during the day can lie down while they wait for parents to pick them up. The area should be somewhat removed from the other children.

Storage Area

An area with cubbies, boxes, or plastic tubs in which children may store their own things. Because SAC programs often share space, these private storage spaces may need to be movable. An area that is readily available to the children is also needed for storing art supplies, small games, and writing materials.

Staff Area

A secure place in which staff may leave their personal belongings, receive messages and information, and take breaks. This area may include comfortable furniture, a phone for staff use, individual lockers, and a cooking and work area for staff.

Administration Area

An area in which to place information files on children and staff, a telephone, first-aid supplies, and other necessities of transacting program business. Some programs may have a separate office; others may have a desk somewhere in the program rooms.

Utilizing the Outdoor Environment

One of the best parts of the SAC program for active school-age children is the opportunity to work off some of their energy outdoors. The outdoor area may be simply a place for children to run and play large-muscle games, but it can be much more than that. The climate in California makes outdoor play a possibility on most days, so you should make as much use of the outdoor area as possible. The outdoor space should be considered an extension of the overall design of program activities, especially if there are periods in your program schedule which call for all children to be outdoors at a given time.

Offer children a variety of activities and choices outdoors just as you do indoors. Consider the following suggestions:

- Take program activities that are normally done inside to the outdoor area. These activities may include art projects, board games, reading, storytelling, or dramatic play (e.g., costumes and props for an outdoor restaurant or farm).
- Use outdoor areas for science discovery activities and experiments, such as building volcanoes in the sandbox or examining small sections of the yard to count the types of life there.
- Provide a water table so that children can engage in math-ematical activities, such as measuring liquids with cups and other containers.
- Increase the variety of outdoor activities to include new kinds of games and equipment, using such items as parachutes, tumbling mats, traffic cones (for obstacle courses), hoola hoops, or bowling balls.

Not all SAC programs have access to large, open grassy areas, such as school playgrounds. Some programs must be more creative in finding places for children to spend time out-of-doors. Even programs that have access to playgrounds may wish to consider alternate areas for a change of scenery now and then. For example, you might be able to walk to a local park—but be sure to increase adequately the number of staff to supervise the children and take the children's emergency cards. Make sure that unusual outdoor spaces are in the direct, visual line of supervision and are approved under licensing requirements.

You need to consider ahead of time the means for transporting equipment to the outdoor play area. Use wheeled carts, net ball bags, or even a sheet with the equipment in the center and the four corners held by different children. Of course, children may help carry equipment and materials when it is safe to do so.

Make sure that new equipment (whether built or purchased) will accommodate children with physical disabilities as much as possible. Apply for grant funding from local service organizations or public agencies to build or adapt existing equipment to meet the needs of more of the children. When designing or purchasing equipment, remember to look at what children with special needs can do rather than what they cannot do.

You may need to adapt some activities to suit limited outdoor space. Consider whether the rules, boundaries, or equipment of traditional games might be changed to accommodate the play area available. Bases may be moved closer together to create a smaller kickball field; tag games may be played by walking or skipping rather than running on parking-lot surfaces; or softer balls may be used for volleyball or basketball in smaller spaces or near breakable objects. Look for new games that are more flexible or that have rules that are suitable for the space you have.

Choosing Materials and Equipment

Some centers may lack sufficient funds to purchase everything that an ideal SAC program would have. Many directors and staff must make choices about the most effective ways to spend the money budgeted for supplies and equipment. Having too few toys, art materials, or other basic supplies creates conflict because children will fight over limited resources. School-age children have a natural curiosity that is at least as boundless as their energy. They need a wide variety of

materials and supplies to try out new ideas and skills and stimulate their growing creativity. You can supplement the supplies your program can afford to purchase by following these suggestions:

- Ask parents and local businesses to save such items as computer paper and colored copy paper used only on one side.
- Join other centers to buy bulk materials at lower cost.
- Creatively recycle such materials as milk cartons (for lightweight building bricks), wood scraps (for sculptures or woodworking), or fabric remnants (for art and sewing projects).
- Submit your request for a specific project to organizations and businesses. Your request should include information on how you plan to use the funds and what your objectives are for the children.

The demands on equipment in SAC programs are far more strenuous than those on the same toy or game in a child's home. Equipment that is popular with children gets heavy use and must be sturdy enough to stand up to it. Inexpensive materials often break or wear out quickly, and you may need to buy the same items several times. The purchase of low-quality materials also changes the nature of children's experience in the program. Using toys that are broken or have pieces missing, scissors that do not cut properly, paper that tears easily, and balls that do not bounce are frustrating for children. The result will be less enjoyment, spontaneity, and creativity among the children.

There are several factors to consider in purchasing and maintaining equipment. When purchasing supplies, consider durability by determining whether there are lots of breakable or losable parts. Consider whether the item will stand up to use by many children each day and whether the item will work properly even if the user is not skilled. To maintain your equipment, plan for proper storage. Protect the equipment by covering it with clear contact paper or packing tape. Gluing joints or double-sewing seams also prolongs the life of the equipment.

School-age children need to be surrounded with materials that challenge their skills and creativity and encourage their involvement. When obtaining materials and equipment, it is important to consider the children's developmental needs, abilities, and interests. Be sure that chairs and tables are the appropriate size for the children in your program. If you serve a wide age range, try to provide for both ends of the spectrum. Select toys and materials that are more complex and open-ended than those used in preschool settings so that children will be inspired to use the materials in creative and individual ways. You should also ask your children what they would like to have in the center. School-age children have a lot of great ideas, and you should consider their suggestions.

A primary concern needs to be the safety of the children in your care. Many problems can be avoided by planning an environment that reduces hazards and encourages safe play. Make checking for broken toys and equipment part of your daily routine and either dispose of broken toys or equipment or set them aside for repair. Impress on the staff and children the need to clean up spills immediately. Post emergency evacuation routes and conduct drills regularly so that children will know what to do in many kinds of emergencies, whether a fire or natural disaster or power and light outages.

In California's culturally diverse population, SAC staff must ensure that their program's environment accurately reflects the language and background of the children in the program. Part of children's sense of belonging in a program comes from seeing around them things that are familiar to their family and background. You can help children develop feelings of belonging in the following ways:

- Understand and respect diversity.
- Use artwork, decorations, items familiar to the children, family photographs, and pictures of the surrounding community in bulletin boards and other displays.
- Address the needs of families who speak languages other than English by translating notices, using photographs, and finding other ways to keep all parents informed of program activities.
- Involve parents in planning and carrying out activities and talk to them about their goals for their children.

Operating in Shared Space

School-age care programs operating in facilities that are used for other purposes during nonprogram hours have a special set of challenges in creating an effective environment. Often these settings are designed for uses that differ greatly from the active and varied curriculum of the school-age program, and staff may have to store all program supplies and equipment used after school, sometimes in locations well away from the program site. When year-round SAC programs operate in schools and children come into the SAC program throughout the day (morning or afternoon kindergartners), the schools may find that outdoor play by SAC children disrupts the elementary school children who are still working in classrooms. The SAC children may need to either play quietly or play in an area away from the classroom, or SAC staff may need to schedule outdoor time at the same time that other elementary children go outside and share outdoor supervisory time. Although these challenges call for staff to be creative and flexible, the difficulties do not preclude operating an excellent program.

One of the greatest challenges in using shared space is the need to dismantle the program in the evening, store the equipment and supplies, and return the materials to the program site the next day. Children in shared-space programs have the same need for variety and choice of activities that all children have, and staff are often frustrated by continual trips to storage areas to gather supplies and materials.

The following ideas may help reduce staff frustration:

- Create mobile centers for art, science, or games by stocking appropriate supplies or equipment on carts that can be rolled into the program and back to storage. Try using the kind of metal cart found in school cafeterias or stacks of plastic crates secured to wheeled platforms or plastic home-storage carts. Be sure the carts are strong enough to carry what you need day after day.
- Label carts holding equipment and materials to indicate the activity areas to which they belong.
- Purchase or commission the building of low wooden cabinets with two or three shelves constructed on casters; the cabinets can be rolled out to use as room dividers in the afternoon and rolled back against the walls at night. If possible, use cabinets that can be locked.
- Schedule sufficient staff time at the beginning and end of the day to set up and store program materials. Children can also be involved in these tasks.
- Continue to lobby for additional on-site storage space as your program becomes more successful. Become friends and allies with the person in charge of your site.

When the basic program facility consists mainly of linoleum, tables, and chairs, you need to find ways to create attractive and workable areas that will convey the possibility and expectation of interesting activities to children. To soften the appearance of the facility and create a warm, inviting environment, try some of the following ideas:

- Use area rugs to set aside portions of the floor on which to sit for activities such as reading, playing games, or using manipulatives.
- Cover tables with oilcloth or vinyl in different colors to designate particular kinds of activities.
- Hang inexpensive and colorful shower curtains to divide areas.
- Create attractive posters to designate different activity areas (e.g., the art area poster might include a collage of different kinds of art equipment or previous art activities). Laminate or cover the posters with clear contact paper and hang them on walls to indicate activity options.
- Use beanbag chairs, throw pillows, futon pads, or gymnastic mats to create comfortable places on which to sit and read or talk.
- Use colorful carpet remnants for seating spaces or for designating activity areas.
- Construct hinged frames that can be covered with bright fabric and used as lightweight area dividers.
- Cover unused or off-limits areas and equipment with patterned sheets or spreads.

Whatever facility you use, it is important for children to see their work displayed and valued. Parents also appreciate seeing their children's work displayed, and the displays make parents more aware of all the activities you are providing. The following are suggestions for creating display areas in shared facilities:

- Use appliance boxes or voting booths as lightweight area dividers on which you can display children's work.
- Bring in rolling chalkboards or easels on which to display work or post notices.
- Tie clothesline to points along the wall; use clothespins to hang pictures for display or to dry. Be sure to put the lines where no one will run into them or disturb them.
- Get donations of colored mat boards from local picture-framing shops to use in displaying children's work and program notices.

Find ways to ensure that children's work will be safe when you say that you will save it. If there is no way to keep projects safe until the next afternoon, save long projects for school vacations.

Creating a Positive Interpersonal Environment

Another important element of the SAC environment is the emotional environment created by children's perceptions of how their needs are being addressed and how people get along together. Children's self-concepts and the interactions among all participants in the program contribute to this interpersonal environment, which is just as important to your program as the physical arrangement of the facility.

Children's Self-concepts

During the early years of their lives, children develop a complex set of concepts about themselves as they begin to define themselves in terms of their skills, preferences, and psychological traits. The self-concept that each child ultimately develops is based on that child's view of his or her capabilities and value in the eyes of others. You can respond to children's increasing independence and ideas and preferences by sending a message to the children that they are capable and valuable. For example:

- Involve the children in the decoration and upkeep of the center so that it becomes *their* place as well as yours.
- Ask the children about the kinds of activities and equipment they would like to see in the center.
- Meet children's growing need for privacy and social interaction by allowing the time and places for children to sit and talk in small groups without adult participation.
- Provide places in which personal possessions can be kept safely.

Positive Interactions

Children's views about themselves and the world are strongly influenced by their interactions with the adults and children around them. Interactions with other children provide the social context for school-age children to sort out what the world is like and how they fit into it.

Staff need to be very conscious of the ways in which they interact with children and how children interact with each other because of the messages that children receive about themselves during those interactions. For example:

- Use a voice level and tone which communicate respect for the child's feelings.
- Make eye contact and use children's names so that the children feel known and valued. But be aware that eye contact is considered disrespectful in some cultures, so find out about the cultural values of your children.
- Talk to children individually, not always to the group in general.
- Help children make friends by encouraging them when they try to socialize or by including a solitary child in a group experience.
- Respond sincerely to children's questions and as fully as time permits.
- Show verbally and nonverbally that you accept and appreciate each child as a valuable member of the program.
- Develop rules with the children about how people are to be treated in your center and enforce the rules.
- Be aware of children who tend to become scapegoats for other children or the target of their teasing or hostilities. Help vulnerable children learn assertiveness techniques and talk with all children about kindness and compassion.

Chapter 5

Managing Your Program

A variety of interrelated tasks and procedures are necessary to manage a program effectively. Procedures include setting program goals, prioritizing and carrying out program tasks, staffing the program, training the staff, and assessing and evaluating program practices. You will need to establish an ongoing process for assessing children's developmental levels, needs, and interests and establish a system for evaluating your program.

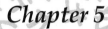

Setting Program Goals

Program management is a process of interrelated activities, not a series of separate events or tasks performed in isolation from each other. The program director, in conjunction with staff, must develop a program philosophy, set goals and objectives for the program that are based on the philosophy, then plan tasks or activities to achieve those goals and objectives. Leaving out any of the management functions may negate positive events.

The job of a school-age care program director is an extensive one and particularly challenging for directors new to the role of managing other staff. The director at the site has a pivotal role in achieving program goals and objectives and in hiring, training, and supervising staff. The director's role is to provide staff members with a clear definition of what is expected of them and the resources and support to help them achieve the program's goals.

The following is a list of interrelated tasks and functions necessary for operating a SAC program. The program's goals and objectives will determine the priorities of these tasks and how, when, and if they are to be carried out. The tasks have been grouped in like functions but they are interrelated, and the director and staff may decide to consider them in a different order or grouping. Some of the tasks may not apply to all programs, depending on the size of the program and the number of sites. The size of the program will also determine whether one or several staff will hold these responsibilities.

Major Tasks and Functions

1. *Management*
   Setting budgets
   Marketing the program
   Emergency planning
   Facility management
   Purchasing
   Food program
   Transportation
   Risk management
   Grant management
   Fund-raising

2. *Children's program*
   Assessing child/family needs
   Behavior management
   Program activities
   Program schedules
   Special-needs inclusion
   Program environment
   Special events
   Program quality evaluation

3. *Staffing*
   Job descriptions
   Staff recruitment
   Candidate interviews
   Staff orientation
   Staff training
   Supervision
   Conflict resolution
   Staff recognition
   Staff evaluation
   Professional organizations
   Contributions to the SAC field

4. *Parent–school–community relations*
   Parent involvement

Parent education
Parent conferences
Family crises
Referrals
Linkages between parents,
school, and community

Once the director and staff have formed the goals and objectives for the program, they need to examine the major tasks and functions in the list above. They need to decide together which tasks relate to the goals and objectives that they have chosen to focus on and prioritize the related tasks and responsibilities for each. They will also have to determine more specific tasks, beyond the major tasks listed above, that are necessary to carry out a particular objective. To prioritize tasks and responsibilities, the director and staff will need to consider the following questions:

1. Which tasks are related to this particular program goal? To this program objective?
2. Which tasks or functions are most important at this site/program?

3. Does our budget plan cover these tasks?
4. Which tasks are highly interrelated and need to be considered together? (For example, budgets are related to purchasing, schedules, and so forth.)
5. Which tasks can be delegated to particular staff members?

An essential part of the process for setting goals and objectives and determining related tasks and functions is to define the major targets of the program.

Defining the Target

As the manager of the program you need to meet with your staff on a regular basis to reassess your program's goals and to evaluate your progress toward achieving specific objectives for those goals. By understanding and participating in the process, staff help make the goals and objectives an integral part of the program rather than simply an impressive statement in the

program brochure. Every staff member needs to be able to describe the program's philosophy, goals, and objectives in serving children and parents. Unless everyone works on the same agenda, program quality will suffer.

One way to analyze your goals (or objectives) is to select a program development topic and draw a target on the board (see Figure 1). You and the staff then analyze what the related program tasks need to be to hit the target (goal or objective), who will be responsible for which tasks, and on what date those tasks must be accomplished.

Then you need to complete a separate graphic representation of the process to show the order of the activities (see Figure 2). This process helps you set priorities, define goals and objectives, and plan the sequence of tasks, rather than allowing the results of the activities to define your program.

The following list gives a brief description of each of the tasks involved in the process of reaching the staff objective of improving tenure and stability:

Job description: What is your program trying to accomplish? What are your targets? The job description you develop should define the job that needs to be done and the personal and professional qualities needed for the job.

Recruitment: How you recruit a person to join your staff will likely determine how that person views both the position and you. Do you believe the person will play an important part in helping the program reach its targets, or is the position for which the person is interviewing not important enough for you to hold your calls and be interrupted during the interview?

Orientation: Are staff given the information they need to know, or do they feel as though they are walking into a mine field? (See Appendix B, "New Staff Orientation Checklist.")

Training: Training should be based on the difference between the level of an individual's knowledge, attitude, and skills and the level of those needs as defined in the job description for the position. (See Appendix C, "Staff Training Assessment and Planning Form.")

Supervision: Supervision involves helping people succeed. It includes timely inspection and correction of performance and respectful two-way communication.

Recognition: Formal recognition includes salary increases, promotions, awards, and letters of commendation. Informal recognition is also important for staff motivation and development and might include words of praise, a note of appreciation, staff T-shirts, or a pizza treat during the staff meeting.

Evaluation: Staff should be given specific, timely, and consistent feedback on how well they are achieving the goals or targets. However, before evaluating someone, it is only fair that you make sure you have communicated what is expected.

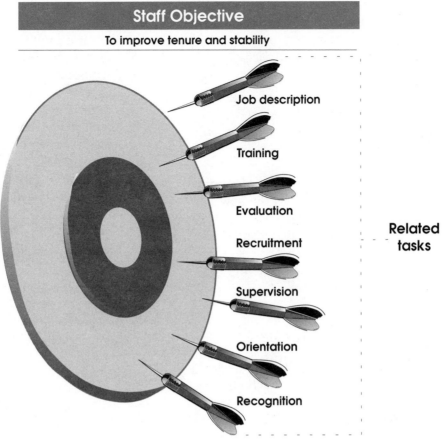

Figure 1

Staff Objective

To improve tenure and stability

Job description

Training

Evaluation

Recruitment

Supervision

Orientation

Recognition

Related tasks

Figure 2

The Process of Meeting the Staff Objective

To improve tenure and stability

Sequence of tasks ▶

Evaluation

Job Description

Recruitment

Recognition

Supervision

Orientation

Training

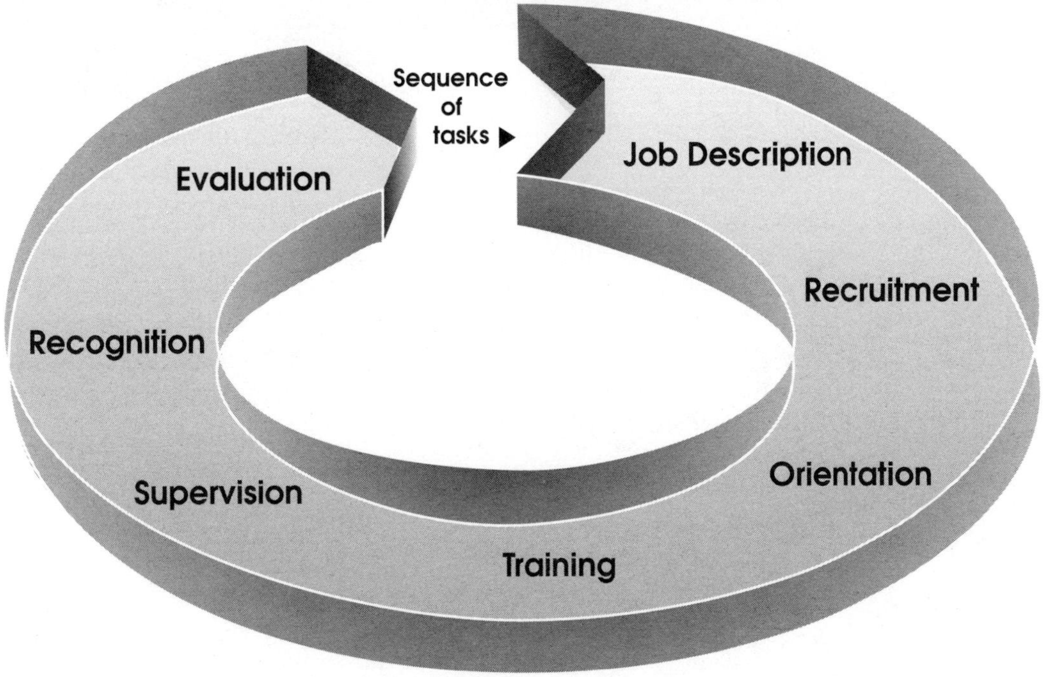

In addition, as a program director you need to ask yourself:

- What happens if you leave out one of the steps identified above?
- Does each of the functions happen only once? (For example, when a staff person's responsibilities change, the person should be recruited again and receive orientation and training for the new assignment.)
- What happens when you do not have clear targets or when the targets keep changing?

Before hiring staff, you need to determine what you want the employees to do and develop a system for determining their ability to perform those tasks.

Program directors and staff are all experts on managing staff because all staff know how they like to be treated. The following sections deal more in depth with the process of selecting staff and improving the tenure and stability of staff.

Selecting the Best Staff

The staff employed to work with children are the key to quality in any SAC program. The particular staff hired by a program will depend on the goals and objectives of the program, affirmative action consider- ations, and the availability of potential employees in that area. If recruitment is a problem in your area, you will need to concentrate more on developing effective staff orientation and training procedures and on retaining good employees after you have trained them. The following considerations will help in identifying appropriate staff and in designing effective ways to train, evaluate, and retain staff members.

Developing Job Descriptions

Before hiring staff, you need to determine what you want the employees to do and develop a system for determining their ability to perform those tasks. Be sure to consider specifics in the following areas: (1) tasks to be performed (e.g., supervision of children, cleaning); (2) planning requirements (informal or written and submitted); (3) supervision responsibilities; and (4) reporting requirements.

Determining Desirable Qualities

It is important to consider the personal and professional qualities of prospective staff members that will enable them to benefit from staff training and become valuable members of your team. Some desirable qualities are as follows:

Personal qualities. A promising SAC staff member:

- ☐ Has strong interpersonal skills.
- ☐ Respects and likes school-age children.

- [ ] Accepts and appreciates individual needs and differences.
- [ ] Has good communication skills.
- [ ] Is reliable and responsible.
- [ ] Shows warmth and caring.
- [ ] Is a good team player.
- [ ] Is flexible and patient.
- [ ] Is positive and optimistic.
- [ ] Is well organized.

Professional qualities. A qualified SAC staff member:

- [ ] Understands the developmental needs of school-age children.
- [ ] Has experience working with this age group.
- [ ] Can maintain confidentiality.
- [ ] Is assertive but not aggressive in dealing with children's behavior.
- [ ] Can select and plan appropriate SAC activities.
- [ ] Is oriented toward professional growth.
- [ ] Relates well to parents.

Recruiting Candidates

Identify several possible sources in your area for recruiting qualified staff members. Some potential sources are local colleges; referrals by other program directors, staff members, parents, or agencies; conferences of professional organizations; professional job banks; school district part-time employees; and classified advertisements in newspapers (try different job categories, such as teacher, child care staff, or recreation leader).

Interviewing Applicants

Use a variety of interviewing skills and techniques to identify and select the most appropriate candidate for your program. Develop a series of predetermined, open-ended interview questions that are based on the job description and create a form

---

It is important to consider the personal and professional qualities of prospective staff members that will enable them to benefit from staff training and become valuable members of your team.

---

to rank candidates on specific issues. Using a set list of questions and a consistent checklist helps to keep interviews uniform and makes the selection task easier. The following are sample interview questions:

1. "What type of art activity would you choose for a group of third and fourth graders?"
2. "How would you handle two children who accuse each other of cheating in a game?"
3. "What do you think is the best thing that we can offer to children in a SAC program?"
4. "How do you feel about working with children from cultural and ethnic groups that are different from your own? Do you have any experience doing this?"
5. "What do you see as your strengths in working with school-age children?"

6. "How do you feel about free play?"

Consider also a *working interview* in which the candidate is paid to "substitute" at your center so that you can observe his or her interactions and skills.

In making your decisions, try to create a balanced staff by selecting people of different ages, genders, cultural and ethnic backgrounds, experience levels, and language fluency and with diverse educational interests and hobbies.

Selecting New Staff Members

Work to select candidates who represent cultural and linguistic backgrounds that reflect the population you serve and will create a balance in your program. Create bridges between ethnic groups by hiring some people who may not be from the cultural mainstream of your program. When choosing candidates, consider their strengths and weaknesses and which attributes are teachable and which are not. Attributes based on attitudes, such as flexibility or patience, usually are not teachable; those based on knowledge or experience, such as understanding a nine-year-old's developmental needs, are teachable.

In making your decisions, try to create a balanced staff by selecting people of different ages, genders, cultural and ethnic backgrounds, experience levels, and language fluency and with diverse educational interests and hobbies.

Orienting New Staff

An employee's first few weeks on the job are the most crucial. If you can provide the new staff person with a successful experience and the knowledge to do his or her job effectively, that person will be more likely to stay on as a loyal employee, thus saving you many hours and the cost of repeating the hiring and orientation process. An additional goal of the orientation process should be to help the new employee become part of your team and feel at home in your center.

Some typical and successful orientation techniques are as follows:

- Developing a plan for providing information on certain topics, such as the location of supplies and equipment, housekeeping issues, behavior management policies, parent communication strategies, emergency plans, and program schedules
- Introducing new staff to existing employees and parents
- Keeping a checklist for each employee so that you can track when information is provided and ensure that none is missed
- Creating a videotaped tour of your center, with an introduc-

tion to your policies, procedures, and schedule
- Assigning a mentor staff person to whom the new staff member can go for answers or tips
- Setting an evaluation conference after the first few months to evaluate progress and set further goals

Supervising the Staff

Clear and consistent policies must be written and maintained on such issues as attendance, punctuality, interactions with children and parents, and professional conduct. Each employee must be made aware of those expectations, and regular conferences should be held to provide feedback on job performance. When staff perform according to expectations, it is important to give them positive feedback on their performance. Using recognition awards and verbal compliments and sharing responsibility for interesting tasks help in supporting staff.

Directors should learn and use proven management techniques to deal with the diverse needs of their staff and program. Techniques such as being consistent, fair, and available, providing support, requiring accountability, monitoring progress, modeling desired behavior, and encouraging staff's continued professional growth are needed as much in SAC programs as they are in other kinds of businesses. Supervisors will benefit by reading material

outside the child care field on this topic.

All staff need a shared vision of the philosophy and objectives of the program to keep them moving toward the same goals. Supervisors must be able to visualize and share with their staff what the program is trying to do for children and their families. Staff meetings, evaluation of events, shared curriculum planning, and group decision

All staff need a shared vision of the philosophy and objectives of the program to keep them moving toward the same goals.

making all contribute to a common vision. It is important also to evaluate the program regularly with the staff to ensure that the decisions that are made support the vision.

Training the Staff

Staff training is a vital part of the growth of quality SAC programs. But it is an area all too easily set aside in the hectic day-to-day pace of programs. Directors must make planning, scheduling, and following through on staff development a strong priority. The topics of the training sessions should be based on needs identified by both the staff and the administration.

There are several methods of providing effective staff training, such as using a section of the staff meeting for training or by arranging special in-house training sessions.

Holding Staff Meetings

The agenda for each staff meeting, published ahead of time, should include a section for training on some issue. The training might take the form of a guest speaker, a presentation by a staff member, a discussion led by the director, or a group problem-solving session. SAC program staff often have a busy, active day and usually are tired when the time comes for a weekly or monthly staff meeting. Therefore, the meetings need to be related to practical topics that have immediate impact on what the staff are doing with the children. The staff usually want more informal meetings that involve discussing some of the problems they are having. However, it is important for the program director also to provide preplanned training that is useful, practical, and professional.

This manual, *Kids' Time: A School-Age Care Program Guide,* could be used in planning your staff meetings and in-house training for the year. Use a different section for each staff discussion; for example, you might discuss "Behavior Management Techniques" in one meeting and "Children Under Stress" in another meeting.

Providing In-house Staff Development Sessions

Directors and coordinators can meet the specific needs of staff at each program site by using parent and staff questionnaires to identify perceived problem areas or gaps in information and skills. Staff members may be used as experts in a given area; outside consultants may be brought in; or directors from other centers may be willing to exchange training expertise.

One of the frequently mentioned obstacles in providing a staff development program is the difficulty in scheduling training because of the varied work and school schedules of SAC staff. Poll your staff to find times that are most convenient. You may have to provide training at different times. Try holding evening meetings with a potluck or dinner, or schedule sessions on Saturdays or during the day when the children are in class. Be sure to make the sessions worth attending and compensate staff for required attendance.

The following are some questions you might ask yourself when planning your staff training:

1. Is one person responsible for and in charge of the staff development program?
2. Has there been sufficient comment from the staff about the training they want and need?
3. Have clear goals and objectives been formulated for this training?
4. Have training dates been announced in advance to respect staff schedules?
5. Is the staff development program planned to meet the individual needs of the staff?
6. Does the staff development program include active participation by those in training?
7. Does the training provide opportunities for the staff to practice the new information in their program activities?
8. Does the training involve support and follow-up activities?
9. Will the staff development program be evaluated by everyone to determine whether the needs of the whole group have been met?
10. Will the results of the evaluation be used to improve and plan for future training?

Selecting Topics for In-house Training

Staff development sessions may be categorized in the following universal topics:

Characteristics and needs of school-age children. This training segment deals with such topics as children's developmental issues, the cultural diversity of the children in the program, children with special needs, and behavior management techniques. Staff need to understand thoroughly what school-age children are like in all areas of development to work effectively with the children. Staff also need to understand that younger school-age children are at different stages of intellectual and social development and that they have interests and hobbies different from those of older school-age children.

SAC staff usually need special training in how to be sensitive to and meet the needs of a culturally diverse group. Part of the training for working with children and families from many different cultures involves learning about the family values and child-rearing practices of the children in the group. Parents and community

Staff must also examine their own attitudes about cultural diversity so that they can consciously eliminate any biases or misunderstandings.

members should be invited to provide some of this training. Staff must also examine their own attitudes about cultural diversity so that they can consciously eliminate any biases or misunderstandings. In addition, the training should help staff become more aware of their own ethnicity and the contributions they can make to the program. The staff should work as a group to make a commitment to being culturally responsive.

A variety of subtopics are related to children with special needs. Attitudinal training deals with imagining what a disabled person experiences, avoiding hurtful labels, and assessing one's own feelings about disabilities. Methods for identifying a child's developmental level and needs include

understanding the Individual Education Plan (IEP) and communicating with parents, teachers, and the child. Other training topics might include techniques for adapting activities for children with special needs; skills and information needed to deal with medical issues; and techniques for dealing with behavioral problems.

Program activities. In this training segment staff deal with forming program goals and planning the activities based on those goals for that program session or year. The training might focus on a particular topic, such as homework assistance skills, positive discipline, or emergency training for earthquakes, if the staff need training on that issue. More in-depth topics might include analyzing the tasks in a SAC activity for children with special needs; analyzing program activities to ensure a balanced, integrated program; relating the presentation of program activities to children's learning styles; or increasing linkages with the school. Some programs develop an ongoing curriculum package or manual of specific activities and train the staff to handle those activities. Other programs develop activities for a week at a time, with opportunities for tapping into children's particular interests that week.

Program environment. This training segment deals with such topics as organizing and caring for the physical environment, both the indoor and outdoor space, and analyzing the program's emotional environment. The group might examine critically certain areas in the facility and decide how to change and improve the space. First, the group should determine what emotional messages the space conveys to the children and whether those messages are appropriate and positive. The environment also might be analyzed to determine whether it meets the program's purposes and is developmentally appropriate and whether the outdoor space is used to its fullest advantage to increase the children's learning.

Parents, community, and the school. The goal of this training is to assist staff in developing strategies to increase the program's communication and partnership with parents and the community. Some of the training would focus on how to communicate through newsletters, program activity calendars, and so forth. Other training might include brainstorming ways to help parents participate in the program or help them support their children's academic work; for example, through tips on how to provide homework assistance. Training may also focus on helping staff understand the parents' concerns and hopes for their child's experience.

Assessment and evaluation. Training in this area focuses on helping staff plan ways to develop an authentic assessment process to use with the children. The training would include developing child observation skills and learning how to set up children's portfolios that include samples of the children's work, developmental profiles, and records of the children's interests and

hobbies. In addition, the staff would learn how to evaluate the SAC program and conduct long-term strategic planning.

Note: Because of the high rate of staff turnover in many SAC programs, training opportunities need to be repeated at fairly regular intervals to train new staff; the repeated topics may serve as refresher courses for continuing staff. Try to use as many different training methods as possible so that staff who are repeating a topic will learn something new or see it in a new way. Besides having speakers make presentations, use different media, such as audiotapes and videotapes.

In addition, staff may be referred to training programs and opportunities available in the community, including attending regional child care conferences. (Contact your local chapter of the National Association for the Education of Young Children, the California School-Age Consortium, or the National School-Age Care Child Alliance to get on the mailing lists for future events.) Other assistance can be found in classes conducted through local university extensions, community colleges, regional occupational training programs, health agencies, social service departments, and school districts.

Evaluating the Staff

To continue to grow and improve, staff must receive feedback on their job performance. In developing a staff evaluation procedure, the director should address the following issues:

1. *Staff evaluations for each employee need to be scheduled on a regular basis.* It is useful to have a probationary period of several months for new staff, followed by a conference and decision on permanent employment. Annual or biannual reviews are often held for permanent employees. Keep in mind that a "surprise" evaluation can be threatening instead of helpful. The reviews should be scheduled on the yearly calendar so that both director and staff can be well prepared and make the best use of this opportunity for growth.

2. *Staff should be part of the evaluation process through the use of self-evaluation forms and mutual problem-solving conferences.* Both the director and staff member may use an evaluation questionnaire to rate the employee's performance, and both may wish to develop goals for future growth. By examining the information together at an evaluation conference, both parties are able to discuss their differences in perception and share comments about goals. Be sure to include discussion on positive performance as well as areas for growth. One outcome of an evaluation conference might be that it helps a staff member make a decision about whether to move to another program or field.

3. *Staff evaluations should be documented and copies given to the staff member and placed in staff files.* Be sure to use written formats for the evaluation to document the issues discussed, goals set, and future action to be taken. This process is especially important when an employee is performing at a less-than-satisfactory level.

Assessing Children's Needs

Children's developmental abilities, needs, and interests should be assessed on a regular basis to learn more about the children, determine their progress, and, if necessary, change the program as a result of the information. Although schools may assess children's development in many areas, such as children's health status and academic achievement, after-school programs need to know and should assess other needs of the children in their care. For example:

• What the children enjoy doing in their free time
• What the children like to eat
• What the children think are their skills and strengths

- What the children already know
- What the children would like to learn how to do
- What skills and concepts the children have learned

Such information is valuable for several reasons. Knowing what the children in your program enjoy and what they would like to learn allows you to plan program activities that meet their needs and provide an enjoyable place for them to be. Being aware of a particular child's feelings and needs helps staff meet those needs in more specific ways. Finding out what children want to do in your program also helps to keep them in the program. Children, especially as they get older, tend to "vote with their feet" and leave the program when it is not a fun place to be. By documenting children's growing capabilities and interests, you are able to share that information with parents and children.

No single method will give an accurate and well-rounded picture of the child. Using a combination of assessment methods produces a more comprehensive assessment of each child. Some suggestions of methods to use are as follows:

1. Include a questionnaire for children and their parents in your enrollment package (see Appendix D). Find out what the children like to do, what some of their favorite activities are, and what they would like to learn at your center. Ask parents for information about their child's favorite activities and what they would like to see their child doing and learning after school.

2. Create a checklist of possible activities that could be done after school and have children rate their top ten favorites. Ask about their favorite snacks, field trips, and other features of your

program. The older children can help design the questionnaire, then help the younger children fill out the form. Older children can also help collate the information and make some recommendations based on their findings.

Encourage parents to add to the journal events that happen at home, such as the arrival of a new sibling or the accomplishment of a new task.

Younger children can share this information with a staff person during a personal sharing time.

3. Keep an individual folder or portfolio for each child and allow staff members, children, and parents to have access to it. Encourage children to add to their folders by writing down special accomplishments or events (such as losing their front teeth or learning a new game or sport), their height and weight on a given day, or things that are important to them; keep the journal page in the folder along with the date. Older children may decide what goes into their folders and set up criteria for determining samples of growth in a particular area. For example, you may suggest that they add samples of their favorite artwork or writing so that they can see how much they

have grown when they look at it later. Staff can add photographs or short notes about observed behaviors or activities. Encourage parents to add to the journal events that happen at home, such as the arrival of a new sibling or the accomplishment of a new task. Keep the folders intact for when the children leave the program, at which time they may take their folders home.

4. Keep a photograph album of children's activities, making sure that you get pictures of all the children in a variety of activities. You might have a new volume for each school year and make the past years' albums available so that children can look back at themselves and their friends, and staff and parents can see how the children have grown physically and how their interests and abilities have changed.

5. Ask the children to reflect on their participation at the end of a group project by considering the following questions: How well thought out was the project? How well presented? What did the group accomplish? What are the strengths and limitations of the project? To what extent did the group work cooperatively to complete the project? The staff might talk with group members to gain this information and tape the discussions, or the staff could ask the children to write about the project, or the group could discuss the project together.

This group self-evaluation can be included in the children's portfolios.

6. Ask children, particularly older children, to assess their own progress in a skill, product, or project. For example, if a child is involved in different art projects during the course of the program, the child could assess the changes or growth made in his or her work. You might take photographs of the children's work throughout the year to help the children assess their progress and confer with individual children about their work. Older children can keep a diary to record their progress. This written or visual information can go in the child's portfolio.

7. Complete observation forms for each of the children as they engage in activities, or write notes on small index cards. You might assign each staff member three children each week and ask the staff to write a paragraph about each child, indicating the activities the child engaged in, the kinds of social interactions he or she had, and the kinds of successes or problems the staff observed. Ask a staff member to observe each child about four times a year in different kinds of activities and keep the results in the child's ongoing file.

8. Document problem incidents or special accomplishments for inclusion in the child's assessment file to help you and your staff see overall patterns of behavior.

9. Add to the child's ongoing file some short documenta-

It is important to assess your program's goals and objectives and current policies and practices on an ongoing basis to plan for growth and change where necessary.

tion of parent conferences or staff discussions of the child and include ideas for meeting the child's needs in the program.

10. Conduct an informal assessment of a child's needs when you talk to parents at the end of the day or during brief telephone conversations with them. Share how a child is doing in specific areas or share growth that you have observed. Be sure to give a balanced report by telling positives as well as negatives or tell more positives than negatives.

11. Include time for more formal conferences with parents at the beginning and end of the year to share information about their children.

12. Link your SAC program assessment with the school's assessment if the SAC children are on the same site. Share portfolio information about individual children with their day-school teachers.

Make assessment an ongoing, integral part of the SAC program, using information gathered at different times and in a variety of quick, simple ways. Look at each child's overall development, not only at problem areas or at growth in a specific area. The child's cognitive, social–emotional, physical, creative, and ethical development are closely linked and should be

The main goal of evaluation should be to facilitate a process of continuing growth for your program by identifying areas of strength and areas that need improvement.

considered as a whole. The information gathered about the children should be used to (1) learn of each child's strengths, interests, and problem areas so that activities can be designed to meet the needs of individual children as well as of the group as a whole; (2) document growth in different areas of development over a period of time; and (3) inform parents and other key people about the child's development.

Evaluating Your Program Through a Self-Study Process

It is important to assess your program's goals and objectives and current policies and practices on an ongoing basis to plan for growth and change where necessary. Practices that have worked well for years may become ineffective as changes take place. For example, changes may occur in staffing, the size of the program, or the population served. The main goal of evaluation should be to facilitate a process of continuing growth for your program by identifying areas of strength and areas that need improvement. Taking the time to look at your program with an evaluative eye will help you to identify current and potential problems before they become crises and to choose the direction of your program.

Each program must find the methods that produce the best results for its unique situation. Consider using one of the following systems as you develop your own method for evaluating your program. Each system has its own program review instrument available for use in your self-study. (See Selected Resources for the organizations and addresses from which to order the following evaluation materials.)

1. *Exemplary Program Standards for Child Development Programs Serving Preschool and School-Age Children*
   Any program may conduct a self-study of its services by using the California Department of Education's *Exemplary Program Standards for Child Development Programs* (EPS). The EPS document contains standards that you can use to measure your program. These quality standards have been

developed for center-based programs and family day care homes serving children from three to fourteen years of age. The quality standards described in EPS have five program components: Environment, Children's Program, Site Personnel, Parent/Site Personnel Partnership, and Administration. The book describes in detail the agency self-study (as well as the validation review) process and how to match each program component and its characteristics with the program being evaluated.

The companion videotape, *How to Conduct Your Agency Self-Study*, is practical and easy to understand. It shows how to conduct a program self-study using the *Exemplary Program Standards* and can be used to train parents, staff members, community representatives, and board members.

2. *Standards for Quality School-Age Child Care*
    A program may conduct a self-study using the *Standards for Quality School-Age Child Care* document developed by the National Association of Elementary School Principals in collaboration with the Wellesley College School-Age Child Care Project. These standards outline the elements of high-quality programs and establish a quality checklist to guide programs through start-

up and improvement by self-study. The key program areas are The Role of the School; Human Relationships; Activities and Time; and Administration. Each program area is evaluated according to specific "Standards of Excellence," with quality indicators that are measurable.

It is important that you have some kind of program evaluation system with which to examine your program to see what is working and what is not working and, therefore, what needs to be changed.

3. *Developmentally Appropriate Practice in School-Age Child Care Programs* and *Quality Criteria for School-Age Child Care Programs*
    A program may conduct its self-study using these two companion documents developed by Project Home Safe of the American Home Economics Association:

    Developmentally Appropriate Practice in School-Age Child Care Programs identifies principles and components of programming that reflect school-age children's characteristics and needs. This publication elaborates on the guidelines and practices for school-age care set forth in the document about developmentally appropriate practice for children from birth through age twelve published by the National Association for the Education of Young Children (NAEYC).

Quality Criteria for School-Age Child Care Programs contains specific indicators of high quality in key program components. Project Home Safe used the accreditation criteria of the National Academy of Early Childhood Programs (a division of NAEYC) as a starting point for its work on SAC quality criteria. The criteria examined are Interactions Among Staff and Children and Youth; Activities/Experiences; Staff-Parent Interaction; Staff Qualifications and Development; Administration; Staffing; Physical Environment; Health and Safety; Nutrition and Food Service; and Evaluation. A program may use this document's more specific SAC criteria to study its own program.

4. *NAEYC Self-Study Materials* The National Association for the Education of Young Children's packet of self-study materials includes accreditation criteria and procedures, a questionnaire, and observation tools. The accreditation process of the NAEYC's National Academy provides an evaluation of programs that serve children from birth through age twelve. The accreditation criteria were revised and expanded between 1988 and 1991 to include more specific criteria for evaluating programs that serve infants and programs that serve school-age children six through twelve years old. This extensive accreditation process involves a self-study and a program review by a

validator who observes the site and verifies the accuracy of the program's description. Programs wishing to do only a self-study may pay an application fee to purchase only the self-study materials.

Evaluation forms that help you examine specific components of your program are also available. *Kids Club* by Linda Sisson and *The Survival Guide to School-Age Child Care* by Betsy Arns contain forms that you may find useful. See Selected Resources for further information on those publications. In addition, you can develop your own questionnaires or surveys to obtain information about particular areas of your program. It is important that you have some kind of program evaluation system with which to examine your program to see what is working and what is not working and, therefore, what needs to be changed.

Use of Evaluation Results

Program evaluation is a growth process. Therefore, the initial evaluation should be followed by the development of goals and methods for achieving the goals or reevaluating old goals. The evaluation results should play a major role in both short- and long-term planning as you proceed with your program.

Evaluation should be ongoing. That is, you need to check constantly with your staff, parents, and children to ensure that the program is operating effectively. Their comments and comments from board members

provide valuable information from a variety of perspectives. See Appendix E for a sample program self-evaluation form for parents. Staff may use weekly or monthly forms to identify briefly things that are going well or to identify problem areas. You should schedule a regular, formal self-evaluation time at least once a year. Define the procedures for your self-study process and let parents, staff, children, board members, and the community know about the procedures.

Once your self-study team has conducted its study using the *Exemplary Program Standards* or other SAC program quality criteria mentioned above, choose two or three areas for improvement that your staff, parents, and children feel are high priorities and which can be addressed with achievable goals. Begin as a group to develop and carry out your action plans. Success in making required changes will fire enthusiasm toward taking on the more difficult projects. Keep track of your goals, the work in progress, and accomplishments. Review these items at each staff meeting to keep your staff moving toward the target. Use the program guide to see if you are progressing toward a high-quality school-age care program. This evaluation process should be followed each year.

An excellent way to use evaluation results in planning for program improvement is through strategic planning. Strategic planning is a technique that was developed at the Harvard Business School and is widely used in both business and educational administration. It is also applicable to SAC planning. The process is broken down into four basic components, which form the acronym S-W-O-T (strengths, weaknesses, opportunities, and threats). To use this process, form a team, preferably one that represents all the groups in your program. The team then participates in brainstorming to make a list of all the ideas that they can think of in each area. When brainstorming, write down all ideas, no matter how farfetched or impossible they might initially seem. Lists such as the following might emerge:

1. Strengths
    -   A staff that really cares about and likes school-age children
    -   A supportive administrative agency
    -   A great group of kids
2. Weaknesses
    -   We are not doing enough science and mathematic activities.
    -   We need to provide more parent education/support.
    -   We need to expand our program for the older kids.
3. Opportunities
    -   Becoming a Regional Occupational Program (ROP) training site
    -   Finding an "Adopt-a-School" partner
    -   Putting on a fund-raising carnival
4. Threats
    -   No money in the budget for staff raises
    -   May not have three rooms next year
    -   Declining enrollment of fifth and sixth graders

With this information your team can start to identify and prioritize problem areas. By identifying weaknesses and threats, you can decide what areas need work. Then you will need to develop an action plan. Part of your action plan to effect solutions will include resources found within the strengths and opportunities categories.

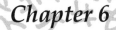

Chapter 6

Establishing Partnerships with Parents, Schools, and the Community

The children served in SAC programs have many facets to their lives. In addition to being participants in the center, the children are also members of a family, students at an elementary school, and citizens of a community. In working to help children become well-rounded, successful, and happy adults, SAC staff must find ways to support and integrate the various areas of children's lives.

The program's goals should strongly reflect parents' goals for their children, and programs must respond to children's growth toward adulthood by helping children become part of the community. Toward that end SAC programs need to develop policies and methods for involving the program with families, schools, and the community and for helping children move successfully between those groups. This final section of the program guide explores these links between the SAC program and the wider world of the children served in the program.

Building Partnerships with Parents

Facilitating parental involvement in SAC programs is often a challenging task. Most parents work during the day and are responsible for homes in the evening. Both children and parents benefit when families feel involved in the SAC program. Before you begin planning in this area, however, poll the parents to assess their needs, their desires, and their ability to become involved.

Encouraging Parental Involvement

Parents need to be involved in the education of their child because they serve as their child's first teachers. With some planning and an awareness of parents' needs, SAC staff can facilitate the educational partnership between the parents and their child, the school, and the SAC program.

By means of parent workshops, verbal communication, and suggested home activities, SAC staff can support those parents who are trying to help educate their child. Staff should encourage the parents to continue the partnership through the child's school years. However, the emphasis must be on fun and informal learning, and the SAC staff need to suggest specific ways to do that. For example, suggest that parents have the child count blue cars when the family takes a trip or write down family recipes to share in the SAC program.

You can involve parents in SAC home-learning activities in the following ways:

- Hold workshops to train parents on the concepts to be developed.
- Emphasize positive, informal, natural ways to learn.
- Ask parents to share traditions, family rituals, songs, and stories with their children.
- Send home necessary materials, such as paper, to create books based on family events.
- Include homework tips or fun learning activities in newsletters to parents.
- Get feedback from parents and children about how the home activities are working.

Try the following suggestions to involve families in school-age care activities:

- Ask parents to contribute to the program by donating materials from home or work, helping with fund-raising or building projects, or accompanying the group on field trips.
- Organize family events at the center, such as potluck dinners or picnics, shows put on by the children, swap meets for children's toys and clothing, or family-movie nights.
- Develop children's projects that involve the family, such as making a family tree or a family scrapbook or doing a survey of family preferences.
- Stage an international fair and ask parents to contribute ethnic foods and decorations.
- Form a parent advisory group that will play a meaningful role in program planning.

Try these ideas to increase parents' attendance and participation in planned events:

- Feature children's work.
- Provide child care.
- Give parents time to chat with other parents.
- Provide a meal or snacks.

Fostering Parent-Staff Communication

Ongoing communication is one of the most important parts of the relationship between parents and the SAC program. After-school programs have an advantage over the school-day program because SAC staff see many of the parents on a daily basis and are able to build continuous, positive relationships and communicate about many issues. However, it is important to

remember that most parents have just finished work and often are tired when they come to the center. Communication about issues that most parents would rather not deal with needs to be handled carefully. Saying something positive about the child when the parents pick up their child at the center is helpful.

To enhance parent-staff communication, acknowledge parents by name and with a smile when they bring their children in and pick them up and send notes to parents about their children. Avoid "jumping" on parents when they walk in the door. Try calling them at home to let them know that you need to speak with them or leave a note in the parent area with some choices of method for making contact, such as "I'll call you tomorrow between 1:00 and 3:00 p.m." or "I'll see you in the afternoon." Create a message system for parents so that they will know where to pick up and leave notes. Some ideas include having a pigeon-hole for each parent in which messages may be placed; providing a message form that parents may leave in a box for any staff member; or leaving a note on the sign-in/out sheet indicating that a message is waiting for the parent.

You might send home a weekly or monthly calendar of events and activities to inform parents about what is happening in the program. The children in the program can use the same calendar to keep track of upcoming activities. This information also helps parents know whether scrounge materials are needed for a special art project and when field trips are planned. Of course, parents' permissions should be obtained prior to any field trips the children may take.

Supporting the Family Unit

Sometimes staff members become so involved in their role in children's lives that they forget the more important role that the child's family plays and may not do their best to support the family unit. When staff are able to help a parent be less frustrated or understand more about effective parenting, staff help children in that family in an important way. Many parents who live away from their own families and support systems find that the staff at the SAC centers are people they can talk to about their problems and people they can ask for help.

There are many small and large ways to help support children's families, whether through direct counseling or by referral to an appropriate community or school resource. Some suggestions include the following:

- Providing or referring parents to classes or workshops on parenting skills or discussion groups on parenting issues
- Encouraging parents to work in the program, when possible, thus helping some to learn new job-related skills
- Maintaining a list of school-linked services, such as counseling, nursing, special education, and migrant services
- Maintaining an up-to-date list of community referral sources

for parents on medical care, counseling, legal aid, shelters, child care, adult education, and community recreational opportunities (Arrange to have your center placed on agency mailing lists for updates on programs.)

- Providing child care services in the evening during workshops and parents' meetings
- Planning a dinner or other service for parents to show your appreciation of their help

Forming Links with the School

One of the common features of all SAC programs is that they serve children who, for most of the year, have spent a large part of their day in a school classroom. Both the school and the before- and after-school programs play important roles in the development of each child. Failing to take advantage of the powerful teamwork possible between the two programs is an unfortunate mistake. A great deal of growth is taking place in both fields as elementary schools take part in school-reform projects, and school-age care programs strive to increase the quality of children's experiences out of school. The commitment to children should lead SAC staff to use all the possible advantages in both fields for the benefit of the children. Forming effective links between schools and before- and after-school programs

enables both to learn from each other and to develop more effective methods for helping the children whose well-being concerns them both.

One of the common features of all SAC programs is that they serve children who, for most of the year, have spent a large part of their day in a school classroom.

Natural Links

Several natural links exist, even when no specific efforts are made to connect before- and after-school programs with school-day programs. These links include the children, the community, and a common site or facility.

Children. The children served in common form the strongest and most consistent link between schools and SAC programs. Even though SAC staff may hear complaints, such as "your children are messing up the cafeteria after school," there is no magical change from "our" children to "your" children when the school release bell rings. The same children who spend their days in the classroom arrive at the SAC program after school. Their basic developmental and personal needs do not change on the way to the SAC program.

Community. The school and the SAC program share a common commitment to be of benefit to the surrounding community. They serve the same parents and must address the same issues that are important to families who live in the area.

Site or facility. In many cases the school and after-school programs operate on the same site and use common facilities. When that is the case, a natural link exists, and the problems that sometimes arise over

Schools and after-school programs have the same ultimate goal—the current and future success and well-being of the children they serve.

shared spaces may be balanced by the benefits of increased visibility, understanding, and communication that can occur between the programs. Teachers and SAC staff have the opportunity for natural communication. For example, an elementary school teacher may go to the SAC program after school to talk with one of her or his students in a more relaxed setting.

Informal Links

There are a few important people on each school campus with whom SAC staff need to establish positive relationships, especially when the SAC program is operated on the school site. These people are the school principal, the school secretary, and the school custodian.

School principal. You will need the support of this person on many issues, such as using the facility and dealing with the concerns of the

parents. Be sure that you impress the principal professionally by doing the following:

- Consider the difference in attire for the two programs and dress accordingly when attending school meetings.

- Keep him or her informed of program activities by sharing the program activity calendar or any special problems that arise.

- Demonstrate that your program has a positive influence on children's growth and development.

School secretary. The secretary is often the heart of the school administration and the center of most information. You will need this person's support to find out about changes in school schedules and to discover the best ways to go about finding people, things, and information. The secretary often has a lot of contacts with parents and may need to answer questions about your program. Enlist the secretary's support in the following ways:

- Learn the secretary's name and show that you appreciate the demands of the position.
- Make sure that he or she has all the information necessary to answer questions about your program and events.
- Do not make extra work for the secretary.

School custodian. The custodian can be a lifesaver or a thorn in your side if you operate on a school site. Get him or her on your side in the following ways:

- Have the children make cards on the custodian's birthday or declare a "custodian thank-you day."
- Share special snacks with the custodian.
- Ask how you can make his or her job easier in terms of scheduling or using facilities.

Establishing a positive and mutually supportive relationship with the elementary school is not always an easy job. There are many constraints, such as lack of time and staff resources, and the philosophies and expectations of the persons involved may differ. However, schools and after-school programs have the same ultimate goal—the current and future success and well-being of the children they serve. The effort put into establishing these links with the school will have a positive payoff for your program, especially for the children who will benefit from the increased agreement between the programs and the shared resources.

Strengths of Each Program

The school and the SAC program excel in many areas that they can share effectively with each other.

SAC program strengths

1. Contact with families is a daily occurrence for SAC staff. That contact facilitates communication and provides a strong picture of the whole child, including family situations, interactions with siblings and parents, and parental concerns.

2. Flexibility to serve the nontraditional learner is standard in SAC programs. Children who have difficulty in the conventional classroom setting because of their personality styles or learning modalities require more hands-on learning and physical activity than is allowed in most classrooms and may be very successful in after-school programs. The same is true of children who have learning disabilities or physical challenges that make schoolwork difficult and frustrating; these children often experience great success in the activities offered in SAC programs.

3. Integrating traditional subject matter areas occurs naturally in after-school programs. The program's projects and activities call for the use of various skills and concepts to produce a result or solve a problem. Children see how such skills as estimating, measuring, problem solving, writing, and crafting are useful in accomplishing something that is significant to them in real life and are not just classroom exercises.

4. A strong focus on social learning and problem solving is at the heart of most SAC programs. The children must learn to play together with children of many ages and cultures or who are different in other ways and must make appropriate choices about their own activities and

behaviors. Because of the structure of SAC programs, children spend a great deal of their time in conversation and interaction with others, including adults, and a significant amount of informal learning takes place as plans are made and problems are solved.

Elementary school program strengths

1. A strong basis in theoretical understanding of learning patterns and instructional strategies is a part of all elementary school teachers' training. School teachers know how to build on knowledge in different fields to form a continuum of learning and how to present information effectively to students.
2. A well-developed language enables teachers to articulate what they are trying to accomplish with children and to discuss their jobs effectively. This professional language is a valuable tool in talking about how to change existing methods to incorporate new knowledge and goals.
3. A system of goals with sequences of activities to meet those goals is accompanied by a great deal of support material to assist teachers in the classroom.
4. A wide variety of resources, such as medical and mental health services, and specialists in such areas as curriculum development and special education are readily available to most elementary schools to help provide appropriate services for most children.
5. A strong focus on developing critical-thinking and learning skills and skills in analysis and synthesis provides a basis for children's future learning and success.
6. A built-in process for professional development days for staff allows them to continue to improve their skills.

Because each program has its own areas of strength and plays an important part in children's growth and education, schools and SAC programs should develop a mutually respectful relationship and cooperate and learn from each other. Both programs can accomplish a great deal in the lives of children by becoming allies and working together.

Methods for Building Links

Try to increase the linkages between school and after-school programs by expanding the communication and participation between both programs.

Communication

1. SAC staff need to understand what schools are trying to accomplish with children. Knowing which skills and concepts are being taught at each grade level helps SAC staff know which skills to include in the fun activities after school. The California Department of Education's

curriculum frameworks also provide useful information on the elementary school goals, programs, and teaching strategies for each curriculum area.

2. Elementary school teachers need to know what the children do in after-school programs. SAC staff should invite the teachers to visit the program when it is in session and include teachers in the distribution of program calendars and newsletters. By referring to the projects and activities done after school, classroom teachers can show children how they are using their academic skills and how to apply new skills.

3. SAC staff and elementary school teachers need to establish liaison representatives from each program to discuss common concerns and ideas. An after-school representative who attends a portion of school staff meetings can open avenues for communication and solve small problems before they become large issues.

4. SAC staff can help children be more successful in school by providing time, space, and homework assistance and by talking to classroom teachers about specific ways to help individual children.

Mutual participation in program events

1. Many training programs and events held by schools and after-school programs may also be of interest and use to the other group. Inviting teachers from both programs to workshops and training sessions requires a little more organizational time, but the increase in information and the opportunity to get to know each other in those settings are worth the effort. Some topics for cooperative training sessions might include "Personality Styles and Children's Behavior," "Learning Modalities," "Hands-on Science

Schools and SAC programs should develop a mutually respectful relationship and cooperate and learn from each other.

Ideas," "Effective Learning Centers," and "Noncompetitive Games for Physical Education." SAC programs may have staff who are able to present some of these workshops and gain extra credibility for the program.

2. SAC staff and elementary school teachers can attend the others' special program events. Such participation builds positive relationships, and children love to see their teachers at their events. SAC staff can attend the school's open house to see the children's class work and meet the teachers. If the SAC program is on site, the staff can open the SAC rooms and

share the SAC program with elementary school parents. SAC staff can also attend school plays or concerts. Elementary school teachers can be invited to attend events staged by the SAC program, or students can invite their teachers to attend a "teachers' tea" at the SAC program after school. The children can serve cookies they have made, and teachers can view the children's projects.

3. SAC staff can often provide useful information on the needs of particular children because they see them in a different setting and often are in closer contact with parents than the classroom teacher is. This information is particularly useful in student study team meetings about children who have special needs. The SAC staff may also want to talk to a child's classroom teacher to develop a united approach in handling an ongoing behavioral problem.

4. The SAC program can become part of the Elementary School District Master Plan and attend planning meetings. In that way the SAC program can enjoy the same benefits provided to the other programs.

5. Sometimes joint purchases of equipment and supplies may be appropriate, especially when programs are operated by the school district and budgets are funneled through the same agency.

6. SAC programs might send a representative to PTA meetings to learn about parents' concerns and issues that relate to the classroom and to answer questions or concerns about the SAC program.

7. Mutual events, such as carnivals, roller-skating evenings, or fund-raising events, can be planned, with each program providing part of the administrative support and "person hours" needed.

Obstacles to Forming Links

Several obstacles may need to be overcome in the process of forming effective linkages. The following are some of the more common problems encountered.

Time. Establishing or improving any relationship takes time, and time is often a limited commodity both in SAC programs and in schools. Despite day-to-day pressures, establishing links should be a priority, and staff should allot time to pursue linkages.

Mutual misunderstanding. School staff may think of the after-school staff as babysitters and view SAC programs as places in which children do little except run around wildly, make lots of noise, and destroy facilities. SAC staff may hold equally inappropriate views of classrooms as places in which children sit constantly in rows, have to be quiet, and do not have fun. The reality is that the boundaries between classrooms and before- and after-school programs are not clear-cut. Elementary teachers are being encouraged to spend less time on skill-based activities for children and to provide more in-depth activities to master the understanding of concepts. The same strategies are used in high-quality SAC programs in which children are encouraged to work together to solve problems, to move beyond basic skills and be creative, and to pursue their interests in projects that spread over days and weeks. Teachers in both programs need to realize that there are valid lessons to be learned from each other and that they have strengths to share, thus setting the basis for valuable communication.

Schedules. Even when SAC programs operate on school sites, communication between the staff members of both programs may be difficult. The SAC staff often arrive at the school when the classroom teachers are leaving, and SAC staff may have other commitments during the day (such as going to school or working in other jobs). When programs operate off-site, the problem becomes even greater. Therefore, time needs to be scheduled for SAC staff and classroom teachers to interact at times that are convenient for both.

Communication/language. One of the reasons for a breakdown in communication and for misperceptions about programs is that SAC staff often are unfamiliar with the professional language of education. The staff may be well versed in child development terminology and still lack the means to

articulate the goals that are being accomplished by activities that look like unstructured play unrelated to any program objectives.

SAC staff usually present program activities and have program goals that are different from those of elementary school teachers or district personnel. SAC staff may have to educate the school district staff on how SAC techniques and goals differ from the teachers' instructional strategies and goals. SAC staff can improve the communication and understanding between the SAC program and the school by

SAC staff can improve the communication and understanding between the SAC program and the school by attending the schoolteachers' meetings and discussing with elementary teachers the SAC program goals related to free play, child-initiated curriculum, and staff-planned curriculum.

attending the schoolteachers' meetings and discussing with elementary teachers the SAC program goals related to free play, child-initiated curriculum, and staff-planned curriculum. When SAC staff, in turn, also learn about the elementary school program, both groups may understand the techniques and goals they have in common as well as where the differences are.

Encouraging Community Participation

Because SAC programs are a part of the wider community, staff need to find ways to create links with the community as well as with the school. The community can be an excellent resource for the program in many ways, and the children need to be increasingly involved in their community as they get older. School-age children are becoming more curious about the world outside their home and school. They want to know how things work, what people do at their jobs, and what their lives might be like as adults.

Children need to be increasingly involved in their community as they get older. They want to know how things work, what people do at their jobs, and what their lives might be like as adults.

They also begin to feel a need to contribute to the community or to the world at large and like to feel helpful. Building relationships between programs and communities also helps children learn about social responsibility and instills in them a sense of pride in their community.

One suggestion for community participation is to arrange for guest speakers (including teachers) to come to your center. There are organizations in every community that serve people with common hobbies or interests. Most people who love doing something love to share that activity with others. Locate businesses and community agencies which have people willing to give presentations of interest to children. These speakers might include local orchestra members, museum docents, college instructors, technology experts, or counselors from local high schools or colleges. By carefully choosing the topic, you can provide an interested group for the speaker and a new experience for the children. You should screen the speaker first by telephone and explain what you would like him or her to do. Another suggestion is to invite community organizations, such as Scouts or Camp Fire, to form groups in your program.

The following are suggestions for finding resources in your community, linking parents with human service agencies, and involving the children in their community.

Finding Resources in Your Community

1. When new families enroll in your program, make a note of their employers. The company may be open to becoming involved when several families from your program work in the company.
2. Contact large companies to describe the kind of resources you are looking for. Do not always think small and ask only for paper or manufacturing scraps. Sometimes large

companies are willing to donate office equipment, furniture, or vehicles that are being replaced because the companies can write off the items in tax reports.

3. Look for prominent community people who may be willing to adopt your program as a good cause and who will bring your needs to the attention of service and social organizations.

4. Be sure you can explain what you are trying to build in your program, what you need, and how organizations can help you. Develop a good brochure about your program for this purpose. The time and money will be well spent.

Linking Parents with Human Service Agencies

1. Find out about all the human service agencies available in the community.

2. Inform parents about the human service agencies. Typically, a parent is at the site daily to pick up his or her child. Verbal communication between staff and parents at that time might lead to a referral to another agency, such as a medical or counseling clinic. Be sure to let parents know of the local child care resource and referral agency, which can supply information about

various family services available in the community. When staff are aware of those community services, they can direct parents with a particular need to an appropriate agency.

3. Help parents link with human service agencies, such as health or mental health services, when these are located at the school site. Talk to the school district administration about the need for these services and the benefits of having them on the school site. Work to become a part of the interrelated services.

Involving Children in the Community

1. Use a map of the city to identify businesses that are within one mile of your center. Contact those businesses to ask if they will permit a limited number of children to tour their facilities, and begin to establish relationships with the companies. Consider various businesses that will be of interest to the children, such as pet stores, car washes, service garages, bakeries, restaurants, or printing companies.

2. Develop community service projects, such as participating in park or school-yard clean-up days and local fund-raising efforts or sponsoring "best yard" contests.

3. Take field trips by walking or by bus. Many areas have small transportation buses that can give a lower group or off-hour rate, but you have to ask for the discount. Remember that not every child has to go on every trip. There are many places to go which can accommodate only a limited number or will be of interest to only a particular group.

4. Have children who feel comfortable doing so participate as entertainers for local groups or as informational speakers on the needs of school-age children, SAC programs, or children with disabilities.

5. Take photographic trips or sketching safaris in your neighborhood. Make texture rubbings, watch birds, collect material for collages, and examine pollution problems.

6. Involve children in an existing community project, such as recycling, reading to senior citizens, or collecting items for a school for homeless children.

By providing links with the child's family, the elementary school, and the community, the SAC program indicates its willingness to become one part of the interrelated services for children, thus helping to coordinate all the needs of the child.

Appendixes

Developmental Stages of the School-Age Child

| Categories | Younger (5–7) |

Cognitive

Display egocentric thinking.

Most children's thinking is egocentric, and children understand the world only from their perspective. It is hard for them to understand someone else's viewpoint, including that of their peers. But they gradually come to understand how other children and adults feel about things if opportunities are presented to discuss others' thoughts and feelings. Children have vivid imaginations and like to engage in pretend play. These children will ask you thousands of questions and are happy doing the same thing over and over again so that they can really learn it.

Demonstrate the beginnings of logical thinking.

During the early school years children undergo a major reorganization in their thinking and begin to think systematically, using several pieces of information to arrive at a conclusion. They also begin to see that reality does not necessarily change, even when appearances do change.

Think logically with the help of concrete objects.

These children begin to think logically as they look at the world around them and interact with their friends, their projects, and their work. These children can hold a couple of concepts in their mind at one time. They begin to understand how something works and why, such as a science experiment, but they still need lots of concrete materials to help them understand. They think more realistically at this time and want the finished product to look real. They like to *work* at something real, such as some kind of job or activity from the adult world. Children at this point sometimes think they know more than adults, partly because they are more skilled and knowledgeable in some areas.

Display natural curiosity.

Their natural curiosity is high, especially as it relates to learning about living things and scientific *whys*. Conducting science experiments and demonstrations, keeping live animals, and exploring outdoors are all popular

Think more like adults.

These children are starting to think like adults. Their thinking becomes more complex, and nothing has one simple answer. They are beginning to do some abstract thinking without needing something in front of them with which to test out the idea. They can see that there may be more than one answer to a problem. They are willing to test out their ideas and make some predictions. They are able to think about what might happen in a situation and are able to do more complex problem solving.

Are interested in the adult world.

Children at this age are becoming interested in political, social, and environmental issues. They can think through complex problems and work through them to arrive at solutions. They will talk for hours about many issues and want to solve the problems of the world.

Lack long-range planning.

These children still lack the ability to think in long-range terms. They do not think about their future and what the consequences of their actions might be.

Cognitive

This ability allows them to play games that involve more thinking and planning than the children did in preschool and to create more involved play activities of their own.

Social-Emotional

Show strong ties between physical and emotional states of being.

Young school-age children often show a strong connection between their physical and emotional states. When they are unhappy or worried, they tend to get stomach-aches or headaches, and when they are excited, they often show activities with this age group. They are able to push forward for further explorations or to search for knowledge. This is a time to take advantage of children's desire to know more about things, and it is important to provide a variety of books and resource materials as well as planned discovery activities to stimulate and address children's curiosity.

Are experiencing a crucial time in school.

School work begins to be an area of great pride or embarrassment for children, depending on the level of success that is being experienced. Children often need adult encouragement to work on homework or academics as the novelty of school has worn off. Children who are having trouble in school begin to fall further behind and often give up at the fourth or fifth grade level without some additional support and encouragement. Many students with learning disabilities are identified at this developmental level.

Begin comparing themselves to others.

At this stage children begin to look at themselves as something more than a combination of their physical traits and start to look at the way they think, feel, and act as unique qualities about themselves. They also begin to com-

Experience mood and energy swings.

Children in this age group are undergoing a great deal of physical growth and hormonal change, which often lead to wide swings between high energy levels, in which they cannot seem to move fast enough or talk loudly enough, and periods of lethargy,

Social-Emotional

it physically by jumping, yelling, or running. These children often forget to pay attention to their physical needs when they are playing and having fun and suddenly discover that they have to go to the bathroom or get a drink of water *right now!*

Have energy highs and lows.

Children in this age group seem to have two speeds, either *high* or *off*. They have tremendous energy and will play hard until they are exhausted, then may fall asleep in a corner. Making the transition from active play to quiet activities can be difficult for this age group, and they may need adult help in balancing their activities.

Begin to play cooperatively.

These younger children are moving from the parallel play of preschool to cooperative play with others in games that involve teamwork and fulfilling different roles. These games often require sharing materials, waiting turns, and engaging in cooperative problem solving, skills which may be difficult for some children until they mature further. Conflicts that arise in these play situations often need staff intervention as children have a difficult time viewing things from another's perspective to compromise and resolve problems.

Have a strong attachment to adults.

In these early years most children are still strongly attached to the pare themselves to other children and adults and think of themselves as more or less capable than their peers. Because of this tendency, children in this age group particularly need support in developing a positive self-image and in identifying their strengths.

Have high energy.

Energy abounds at this stage, and the children require a great deal of sleep. They sometimes become overstimulated in active or competitive activities.

Are able to learn from each other.

As they mature and learn new skills, children are more able to help each other learn. They can work with other children, particularly those younger than they, to teach a skill or concept that they have mastered themselves by using demonstration and explanation techniques. Children in this age group can work well with younger children and often enjoy the role of teacher.

Develop relatively stable groups of friends.

Children in this age group tend to form friendships or play groups that remain fairly stable, even though they may argue with their friends frequently. Girls tend to play together in smaller groups than boys and tend to place a high priority on sharing secrets and giving mutual support. The desire

when they want to do nothing but sit and talk or read or stare off into space. Along with these sometimes rapid changes in energy level, swift and intense changes in mood or emotion will be evident. When they are happy, these kids are ecstatic, jokes are hilarious, and everything is fantastic. When they are unhappy, they plummet into a world that is "terrible," in which no one likes them or will ever like them again. Almost as suddenly, they can shift back.

Require limits.

Preadolescents often feel that since they are so old and wise, they should be immune to most rules and limitations. Children need to feel they have had a part in creating limits they perceive as reasonable. These limits must then be enforced calmly and consistently. If the children think that the rules or staff can be manipulated, they will usually do their best to do so. Children this age need to be reminded of the rules (because they really do forget almost as often as they say they do) and need to have consequences enforced in a firm, fair, and friendly manner.

Have a need for privacy.

This is an age when children want to feel that they are old enough not to need supervision constantly. They need to have a feeling of privacy and trust within the structure of a program. They need to understand the conditions for earning and retaining

Social-Emotional

significant adults in their lives and need a lot of affirmation and affection from them. Getting attention from staff may be a strong motivator for young children, and they use a variety of techniques, based on what they have discovered to be effective, to get that attention

Have an emerging sense of humor.

Young school-age children love to tell jokes, even though they are often long and frequently not funny to adults. Their jokes are often based on a lack of skills that they have recently learned themselves, such as a person forgetting his or her phone number. Telling jokes and easy riddles strengthens their language skills in a fun way. Children's jokes and stories may seem to go on forever without a punchline.

Have limited control of expression.

Control over their emotions and their means of expressing their feelings is often limited in these younger children. They may be loud in their play and in their responses and often need reminders as they learn to control their voices. They may also have difficulty in making the transition from reacting physically to frustration to expressing themselves orally. They may need lots of encouragement to finish projects that are not turning out right or help in settling conflicts with others.

Are developing their self-identity.

In their early interactions with the wider world of their school and to belong to a group is strong, and team sports and clubs with a group goal are popular at this age.

Have extreme reactions to many things.

Children in this age group may appear to have mood swings because of their extreme reactions to people and situations. They often get very angry and frustrated about being teased and find it difficult to follow staff's advice to "just ignore it." Staff need to help all children learn to identify and deal with their feelings and should try to help groups talk about how it feels to be teased and how to handle teasing. On the other hand, when children of this age are happy or upset, there is often no doubt about it because of their loud and often physical ways of expressing themselves.

Are making critical choices about gangs and drugs.

This is a period during which many children are making critical choices about involvement in substance abuse, sexual activity, and gangs. Children at this age need to learn about making decisions that will be good for their lives and how to deal with peer pressure. Self-esteem-building activities will also help children to avoid many of these potentially self-destructive behaviors.

Exhibit growing independence.

These children are often becoming more independent in their thinking

those privacy privileges and should be allowed to try them out a few at a time to learn how to handle them.

Engage in power struggles.

At this time in their lives, many children feel as powerless as they ever will. Preadolescents often are not given most of the freedoms that they want. They have little say in issues that are important to them, such as observing curfew or deciding on whether or not to go to school; have very little money since they cannot work; and are still dependent on others for their transportation. To gain some feeling of control, they often will engage in power struggles with the adults who must enforce limits.

Need to develop self-esteem.

This age brings on the most self-criticism and self-doubt compared to any other age. Preadolescents are constantly comparing themselves with everyone else around them and usually find themselves lacking in any number of ways. They want to be taller, skinnier, smarter, better at basketball, prettier, more of something, or less of something than they are. They are sure that everyone is looking at them with the same critical eye and that somewhere, someone is laughing at them.

Experience relationship traumas.

One of the most important things to most preadolescents is their relationship to their friends. Unfortunately, because there is so much change

Social-Emotional

community, children begin to develop a picture of themselves and how they relate to the culture and language of their families; the ethnic differences between themselves and their peers; and the way to deal with these issues. They also continue to learn about their roles as girls and boys and to develop ideas about social expectations for their own and the opposite gender.

Want to be part of older children's activities.

Activities in which older children engage always seem to be the most attractive to the younger children. They want to break through the bonds of being a "little kid" and get on with life. They admire the older children and want to emulate them.

Need assistance with transitions.

These younger children, especially kindergartners, need some extra assistance and patience from staff in learning the rules and schedules of the program. Younger children also need more guidance and comfort as they get oriented to a new home or school and a before- and after-school program.

and proud of their ability to plan and carry out ideas. This age group needs lower-profile supervision than younger children and time to create their own activities. If adults participate too much, children will often stop their play and go on to something else.

Are able to work in groups.

These children usually like to work in groups with other children. Formal teamwork is possible among them, and they begin to see themselves as workers.

taking place, many friends begin to move in new directions and outgrow each other. It is very hard for these children to see themselves losing a friend with whom they have been very close. Conflicts also arise between friends when mood swings do not coincide or when self-doubts lead one friend to sacrifice the other to gain acceptance or move the spotlight onto someone else.

Physical

Have gross motor skills.

These children are graceful and skilled physically. Most can ride a bicycle, climb a ladder, pump a swing, and throw, catch, and kick a ball. Some can skate and ski, activities that require balance and coordination. Almost any gross motor skill that does not require much strength or judgment can be learned by this age group.

Are developing fine motor skills.

Fine motor skills, such as cutting food with a knife and fork or printing with a thin pencil, are still difficult for this age group. Many of these children have not developed the muscular control or careful judgment needed for fine motor skills, particularly since they may still have short, fat fingers.

Like to practice their motor skills.

Most young children practice their motor skills wherever they are, whether climbing ladders or balance boards in the SAC program or climbing fences in the neighborhood. They are constantly on the move, practicing their skills by teaching themselves and learning from other children. Games that young children love, such as tag, seem designed to accommodate children with different physical abilities.

Begin exhibiting physical differences.

Physical differences between children are becoming more apparent, and wide variations in size and shape may emerge among children of the same age group. Children who find themselves on either end of the size spectrum may have problems at this age as smaller children may be teased and larger children may be labeled as the group protector.

Develop physically at a smooth and uneventful rate.

Most children continue to master new physical skills quickly, provided they have the opportunity to practice them. However, boys begin to have an advantage over girls in nearly all physical activities. These children grow more slowly than they did at the younger age or than they will in preadolescence. The average child grows thinner while getting taller, and muscles become stronger. But many healthy children are much larger or smaller than average.

Can make social problems out of physical difficulties.

Children's bodies at this age may become a source of embarrassment to them. Children become more aware of their peers' opinions and are more likely to react to differences no matter how small. Those children with physical problems, including such minor ones as needing glasses, may be teased or made to feel uncomfortable.

Show great hormonal changes and physical growth.

Children at this time enter puberty and begin to reach adult size and shape and their primary and secondary sexual potential. They develop definitive male and female sexual characteristics.

Begin a period of rapid physical growth.

Children in this age group begin a period of rapid physical growth, generally referred to as the growth spurt. The growth spurt begins with a rapid weight gain. Then a height spurt begins. However, girls usually experience the accelerated growth of puberty approximately two years before boys, causing the girls to be taller during that time.

Often experience a period of great adjustment.

Often, great physical and hormonal changes cause great adjustment for the children, their families, the teachers, and SAC staff. The changes may lead to a time of child-parent bickering and a lack of self-confidence for the children, all of which the children usually outgrow.

Physical

Creative

Dance

In this age group children are developing an awareness of their bodies as a source of potential movement and like to experiment in doing different things with their bodies as they sway and move. They can talk about how the movement feels and can create a simple dance with a beginning and ending.

Music

The children like to sing songs with simple melodies and improvise simple tunes and rhythms while they use their voices, bodies, or musical instruments. They like to experiment with simple percussion instruments, such as drums, and tonal instruments, such as melody bells.

Compare their physical skills with those of their peers.

Acquiring physical competence among their peers becomes important at this stage. These children compare themselves with each other, and those behind in physical development or skills sometimes feel inadequate. Physical development during this period even affects friendships, which become based, in part, on physical appearance and competence.

Dance

The older children continue to enjoy experimenting with their bodies through movement but are also interested in learning a variety of dances, including solitary ones, those with partners, or group dances. They get quite skilled at some of these dances and like to participate in group dances, such as square dancing. However, some of the children become self-conscious, and often the boys and girls pair up with the same sex to do these dances.

Music

The children like to sing rounds, descants, and songs in two or more parts. They like to sing alone or in a group. They can play simple melodies on different instruments, such as bells, or play chords on such instru-

Dance

Many of the oldest children are highly skilled dancers. They can improvise and make up their own movements and steps or do the latest dances. They may compare dances and analyze them in detail. The boys and girls are sometimes shy dancing together so girls sometimes still dance with girls. It is important for them to learn the latest dances to do in front of their peers.

Music

Most children really enjoy all kinds of music; preferences depend on the individual and his or her culture and experience. They like to listen, sing, and dance to music, particularly to the current tunes on the radio. They

Creative

Art

Children at this age like to experiment with a variety of art media, including painting, drawing, construction, printmaking, and crafts. They like to select, arrange, and make decisions about the art projects with which they are involved. They are less concerned with the final product than with their experiments with the media and materials. They like to do crafts, such as weaving or stitchery, but are just learning the beginning levels of the crafts.

Theater

The children like to engage in simple sociodramatic (let's pretend) play in which they take on roles related to the familiar adult world. They like to use props, both real or replicas, to further their fantasies and develop their imaginations. They constantly talk as part of their roles.

ments as autoharps or guitars. They can create compositions and interpret standard notation.

Art

Children continue to experiment with a variety of art media and processes, such as graphics. They have increased their skills in working with these media and can do techniques such as shading and brush drawing. They are interested in their finished products and like to critique them carefully. They are able to make realistic and more abstract objects. Some become quite skilled in such crafts as construction, stitchery, batik, and jewelry.

Theater

Children at this age like to develop story dramatizations and can improvise stories. They can write plays individually and cooperatively based on their imagination and experiences. They like to put on plays and develop all the props and costumes.

have their favorite singers and groups and know the current rock, rap, and country singers and buy their tapes. Some children attend concerts. Some play instruments and play them very well. Some children are able to perform alone and in a group, and some even write their own compositions.

Art

Children in this age group are able to draw and paint at a high level when that is their particular interest and talent. They can be able craftspersons, with a control over the medium and techniques required. Many like to do very intricate designs, such as graphics creating optical illusions with spatial impact. The children at this age take great pride in their work and carefully critique and analyze their finished personal work or group project. The children can identify and discuss works of art selected from various American ethnic backgrounds, show variations in style, and take pride in their own ethnic artwork.

Theater

Children in this age group who are interested and active in the theater can be sophisticated performers. They can create and perform pantomimes; present comic subject matter; tell stories to others with a dramatic impact; memorize and present scenes from plays; write, produce, and direct their own plays; or produce existing plays.

Ethical

Believe rules are sacred but do not always play by them.

These children tend to think that rules are sacred and unchangeable but tend to apply them in an egocentric way. The children may apply the rules of a game differently as the game goes along, acting on their own feelings or whims rather than on rules formed by mutual consent. They often play games with little regard for the rules.

Think it is unfair to do what is forbidden.

Children think it is unfair to tell lies or to "make a noise with your mouth in school." They think it is unfair for one child to be given an apple bigger than that given to another child. Their ideas of fairness are tied to unequal treatment but at a concrete, personal level.

Believe in obeying authority figures so they do not get punished.

Children at this age often obey the rules because of fear of punishment from adults, not because they understand at any deep level what is right or wrong. They also obey the rules or are nice to someone so that person will be nice to them, rather than because it is the right or ethical thing to do.

Play by the rules.

Children at this age play by the rules in their games. They respect the rules and want to learn them to play their games correctly. They think it is wrong if other children go against the rules of the game they are playing. However, they also come to understand that rules can be changed, if warranted.

Believe in social, conventional rules.

They believe that good behavior is that which pleases other people and wins their praise, so they try to be "good kids." They believe strongly in law and order.

Believe in fair treatment.

They think it is unfair if one child or person is treated better than another. This is very important to them. They do not like it if two children do the same work and one gets a reward for it and the other does not. For instance, they might fight over who gets to help the staff clean the room.

Begin to make ethical decisions by themselves.

These children begin to examine and reflect on social and ethical issues and think deeply about them. They look at the implications of their moral decisions.

Think social injustice is unfair.

Social injustice becomes very important to these children, and they become strongly interested in righting some of the wrongs in society or their community. They are willing to work for a cause and might like to work at their level in some sort of advocacy project. For instance, they would be happy and very involved in working on a project to collect food for the homeless.

Are willing to revise outdated rules.

They believe that rules exist to help everyone and that everyone must mutually agree on them. However, if the rules become hurtful, or everyone in the group (such as their group of peers) does not live up to them, then the children are willing to break or change the rules.

Note: This text on the ethical development of children is adapted from the moral development theories of Jean Piaget (1962) and Lawrence Kohlberg (1963), quoted in *The Developing Person Through the Life Span* (Third edition), by Kathleen S. Berger. New York: Worth Pubs., Inc., 1994.

Appendix B
New Staff Orientation Checklist

Employee: _____   Supervisor: _____

Date of Employment: _____

I. Job Definition

_____Discuss the program mission, philosophy, and unique features of the job.

_____Review and discuss the job description.

_____Identify and discuss priorities for the next three months.

_____Discuss specific standards of performance/expectations.

_____Identify present level of skill and understanding of all phases of job assignment.

_____Identify people who might be helpful in learning skills and routines.

_____Encourage new staff to read program manuals and resources.

_____Review licensing regulations and requirements.

_____Review the California Department of Education's *Exemplary Program Standards.*

_____Review requirements for necessary certification: first aid, CPR, driver certification, college units.

_____Discuss career development opportunities and training.

_____Set specific times to meet together.

II. Personnel Policy and Required Practices

_____Review the agency's personnel policy.

_____Review policies and safety practices related to specific areas.

_____Review sign-in/sign-out procedures.

_____Review forms and due dates related to payroll, reimbursement for expenses, and insurance and retirement forms, if applicable.

_____Discuss emergency care and the program's disaster plan.

_____Review the program's budget and staff accountability.

III. Staff, Parents, and Volunteers

_____Introduce agency staff and discuss their responsibilities and authority.

_____Identify key parents, community leaders, and agency volunteers.

_____Support attendance at meetings of related groups: parent advisory committee, agency board or committee, and PTA.

_____Review dates and format for staff meetings.

IV. Mechanics

Familiarize new staff with:

_____Office procedures and capabilities

_____Purchase orders

_____Petty cash

_____Files

_____Telephones

_____Xerox machines

_____Office supplies

_____Program supplies and the inventory system

_____Accident forms

_____Audit trail requirements

V. Facility

_____Acquaint new staff with the building's layout: lights, heating, air conditioning, fire alarm, supply storage.

_____Assign keys and review the lock-up procedure.

_____Review fire extinguisher usage and location.

VI. Community

_____Provide information on geographic, social, and political aspects of the community.

_____Provide information about other community programs and services.

_____Arrange introductions to staff involved in interagency and school district partnerships.

Appendix C

Staff Training Assessment and Planning Form

Training plan for: _____   Date: _____

Supervisor: _____   Child care site: _____

1. Review the knowledge and skills needed for the position as defined in the job description. In which areas does the staff person need additional training (as determined by the supervisor and staff person)?

    a.

    b.

    c.

    d.

    e.

2. Identify in-service training events or staff meetings at the agency that relate to the areas noted above.

Training event	Date	Time

3. Identify additional training events required by the agency or for community care licensing.

Training event/class	Date	Time	Cost

4. Identify training events suggested by the staff person or agency that would provide opportunities for personal growth or career advancement.

Training event/class	Date	Time	Cost

    Total days needed: _____   Total cost: _____

Appendix D

Parent Intake Survey

Child's name: _____   Date of birth: _____   Age: _____

School attending: _____   Teacher: _____

Parents' names: _____

Home telephone: _____   Work telephone: _____

1. Child care needs

    Before-school hours: _____ to _____   M T W TH F

    After-school hours: _____ to _____   M T W TH F

    What previous child care services have you used? _____

    _____

2. What are your child's special needs, if any?

    Physical: _____

    Medication: _____

    Food allergies or diet restrictions: _____

    Special services from the district: _____

    How can we best meet the needs of your child?
    (i.e., child's likes, dislikes, fears, concerns)

3. What activities does your child most enjoy doing?
   (i.e., interests, skills, talents, hobbies)

4. How long will your child spend at an activity he or she enjoys?

5. Can your child express himself or herself orally so that others are able to understand him or her? If not, how does your child communicate with others?

6. What techniques are effective when your child is upset?

7. How does your child tend to enter into group experiences?

8. Please give us any other information that you feel would be helpful for staff to know about your child.

Appendix E

Parents' Program Evaluation Survey

Dear Parents:

We, the staff of the school-age care (SAC) program, are inviting parents to express their views of our program through the completion of this questionnaire. Your responses will help us in evaluating your SAC program and assist us in planning for the future. We would appreciate it if you would complete this questionnaire by _____ and return it to the SAC offices. Your responses will be kept strictly confidential. Thank you.

1. Please rate the following factors based on your level of satisfaction with the SAC program:

	Very satisfied	Satisfied	Dissatisfied	Very dissatisfied
Activities	_____	_____	_____	_____
Facilities	_____	_____	_____	_____
Staff	_____	_____	_____	_____
Fees	_____	_____	_____	_____
Morning hours	_____	_____	_____	_____
Afternoon hours	_____	_____	_____	_____
Learning environment	_____	_____	_____	_____
Overall program quality	_____	_____	_____	_____
Snacks	_____	_____	_____	_____

2. Will your child be using the SAC program at the elementary school level next year?
    ( ) yes   ( ) no   ( ) maybe   ( ) don't know

3. How many children do you have in the SAC program now?
    ( ) 1   ( ) 2   ( ) 3   ( ) 4   ( ) 5 or more

4. What grades are your children in (check all that apply)?
    ( ) kindergarten   ( ) second   ( ) fourth   ( ) sixth   ( ) eighth
    ( ) first   ( ) third   ( ) fifth   ( ) seventh

5. What SAC site does your child attend?

_____

_____

_____

_____

6. Did your child receive a transfer to attend this school?

( ) no   ( ) yes   If yes, from which school/district? _____

7. Do you receive public funding?

( ) yes   ( ) no

8. Your marital status:

( ) married   ( ) single   ( ) divorced

( ) separated   ( ) widowed

9. You are the child's:

( ) mother   ( ) guardian

( ) father   ( ) other

10. Additional Comments:

_____

_____

_____

_____

_____

_____

Thank you for filling out this questionnaire. Please return it by _____. You may mail it to:

_____

_____

_____

Selected Resources

Printed References

CHAPTER 1

General Resources

Albrecht, Kay M., and Margaret C. Plantz. *Developmentally Appropriate Practice in School-Age Child Care Programs* (Second edition). Dubuque, Iowa: Kendall/ Hunt Publishing Co., 1993.

Arns, Betsy. *The Survival Guide to School-Age Child Care.* Huntington Beach, Calif.: School-Age Workshops Press, 1988.

Baker, Nancy A. *Strategies for School-Age Child Care in Texas* (Revised). Austin, Tex.: Corporate Child Development Fund, 1991.

Bender, Judith Schuyler-Haas; Barbara Elder; and Charles Flatter. *Half a Childhood: Time for School-Age Child Care.* Nashville: School Age Notes, 1984.

Bergstrom, Craig, and Joan M. Bergstrom. *All the Best Contests for Kids, 1992–1993* (Third edition). Berkeley, Calif.: Ten Speed Press, 1992.

Developmentally Appropriate Practice in Early Childhood Programs Serving Children from Birth Through Age 8. Edited by Sue Bredekamp. Washington, D.C.: National Association for the Education of Young Children, 1987.

Exemplary Program Standards for Child Development Programs Serving Preschool and School-Age Children. Sacramento: California Department of Education, 1991.

Military Child Care Project. *Caring for School-Age Children.* Washington, D.C.: Superintendent of Documents, U.S. Government Printing Office, 1980.

Quality Criteria for School-Age Child Care Programs. Edited by Kay M. Albrecht. Alexandria, Va.: Project Home Safe, American Home Economics Association/ The Whirlpool Foundation, 1991.

Richard, Mary M. *Before and After School Programs.* Nashville: School Age Notes, 1991.

The Right Place at the Right Time: A Parent's Guide to Before- and After-School Child Care. Alexandria, Va.: National Association of Elementary School Principals, 1993 (brochure).

Seligson, Michelle, and Michael Allenson. *School-Age Child Care: An Action Manual for the 90's and Beyond* (Second edition). Westport, Conn.: Greenwood Publishing Group, Inc., 1993.

Sisson, Linda. *Kids Club: A School-Age Program Guide for Directors.* Nashville: School Age Notes, 1991.

Standards for Quality School-Age Child Care. Alexandria, Va.: National Association of Elementary School Principals, 1993.

Chapter 2

Special Needs

Bissell, Joan S., and others. *School-Age Care for High-risk, Substance-exposed Children.* Sacramento: California Department of Education, forthcoming.

Cook, Ruth E., and others. *Adapting Early Childhood Curricula for Children with Special Needs* (Second edition). New York: Macmillan Publishing Co., 1987.

Fink, Dale. *School-Age Children with Special Needs: What Do They Do When School Is Out?* Boston: Exceptional Parent Press, 1988.

Froschl, Merle, and others. *Including All of Us: An Early Childhood Curriculum About Disability.* New York: Educational Equity Concepts, Inc., 1985.

Souweine, Judith, and Sheila Crimmins. *Mainstreaming: Ideas for Teaching Young Children.* Washington, D.C.: National Association for the Education of Young Children, 1981.

Staff-Child Interactions

Chase, Larry. *The Other Side of the Report Card: A How-to-Do-It Program for Affective Education, Grades 4–6.* Glenview, Ill.: GoodYear Books, 1975.

Faber, Adele, and Elaine Mazlish. *How to Talk So Kids Will Listen and Listen So Kids Will Talk.* New York: Avon Books, 1982.

Gibbs, Jeanne. *Tribes: A Process for Social Development and Cooperative Learning* (Revised edition). Santa Rosa, Calif.: Center-Source Publications, 1987.

Kaufman, Gershen, and Lev Raphael. *Stick Up for Yourself! Every Kid's Guide to Personal Power and Positive Self-Esteem*. Minneapolis, Minn.: Free Spirit Publishing, Inc., 1990.

Kreidler, William J. *Creative Conflict Resolution*. Glenview, Ill.: GoodYear Books, 1983.

Therrell, Jim. *How to Play with Kids: A Powerful Field-Tested Nuts and Bolts Condensed Guide to Unleash and Improve Your "Kid-Relating" Skills* (Revised edition). Austin, Tex.: Play Today Press, 1992.

Theoretical Framework

Baldwin, Bruce A. "The Fundamentals of Play," in *Beyond the Cornucopia Kids: How to Raise Healthy Achieving Children*. Wilmington, N.C.: Direction Dynamics, 1993.

Berger, Kathleen S. *The Developing Person Through the Life Span* (Third edition). New York: Worth Pubs., Inc., 1994.

Cortez, Carlos E. "Multicultural Education: A Curricular Basis for Our Multi-Ethnic Future," in *Doubts and Certainties: Working Together to Restructure Schools*. Edited by Peter A. Barrett. Washington, D.C.: National Education Association, 1991.

Derman-Sparks, Louise, and the A.B.C. Task Force. *Anti-Bias Curriculum: Tools for Empowering Young Children*. Washington, D.C.: National Association for the Education of Young Children, 1989.

Erikson, Erik H. *Childhood and Society*. New York: W. W. Norton and Company, Inc., 1993.

Gardner, Howard. *Art, Mind, and Brain: A Cognitive Approach to Creativity*. New York: Basic Books, Inc., 1984.

Gardner, Howard. *Frames of Mind: The Theory of Multiple Intelligences* (Tenth anniversary edition). New York: Basic Books, Inc., 1993.

Growing up Learning. Edited by Walter B. Barbe. Herndon, Va.: Acropolis Books, 1985.

Health Framework for California Public Schools, K–12. Sacramento: California Department of Education, 1994.

Katz, Lillian; D. Evangelou; and J. A. Hartman. *The Case for Mixed-Age Grouping in Early Education.* Washington, D.C.: National Association for the Education of Young Children, 1990.

Kohlberg, Lawrence. "Development of Children's Orientation Toward Moral Order" (Part I). Sequence in the Development of Moral Thought. *Vita Humana,* Vol. 6 (1963), 11–36.

Moral and Civic Education and Teaching about Religion. Sacramento: California Department of Education, 1991.

Physical Education Framework for California Public Schools, K–12. Sacramento: California Department of Education, 1994.

Piaget, Jean. *The Moral Judgment of the Child.* New York: Free Press, 1965.

Piaget, Jean. *Play, Dreams and Imitation in Childhood.* New York: W. W. Norton and Co., Inc., 1962.

Piaget, Jean. *Psychology of Intelligence.* Lanham, Md.: Littlefield Adams Quality Paperbacks, 1976.

Van Hoorn, Judith, and Pat Nourot. *Play at the Center of the Curriculum.* New York: Macmillan Publishing Co., 1992.

Visual and Performing Arts Framework for California Public Schools, K–12. Sacramento: California Department of Education, 1989.

CHAPTER 3

Curriculum Resources

Blakeley, Barbara, and others. *Activities for School-Age Child Care* (Revised edition). Washington, D.C.: National Association for the Education of Young Children, 1989.

English–Language Arts Framework for California Public Schools, K–12. Sacramento: California Department of Education, 1987.

Gardner, Howard. *The Unschooled Mind.* New York: Basic Books, 1993.

Gork, Mardi, and David Pratt. *Activities for Before and After School.* Nashville: Incentive Publications, Inc., 1991.

Haas-Foletta, Karen, and Michele Cogley. *School-Age Ideas and Activities for After-School Programs.* Nashville: School Age Notes, 1990.

Health Framework for California Public Schools, K–12. Sacramento: California Department of Education, 1994.

Here They Come: Ready or Not! Report of the School Readiness Task Force. Sacramento: California Department of Education, 1988.

History–Social Science Framework for California Public Schools, K–12. Sacramento: California Department of Education, 1988.

It's Elementary! Elementary Grades Task Force Report. Sacramento: California Department of Education, 1992.

Katz, Lillian, and Sylvia C. Chard. *Engaging Children's Minds: The Project Approach.* Norwood, N.J.: Ablex Publishing Corp., 1989.

Mathematics Framework for California Public Schools, K–12. Sacramento: California Department of Education, 1992.

Physical Education Framework for California Public Schools, K–12. Sacramento: California Department of Education, 1994.

Science Framework for California Public Schools, K–12. Sacramento: California Department of Education, 1990.

Visual and Performing Arts Framework for California Public Schools, K–12. Sacramento: California Department of Education, 1989.

CHAPTER 4

Physical Environments

Greenman, Jim. *Caring Spaces, Learning Places: Children's Environments That Work.* Redmond, Wash.: Child Care Information Exchange, 1988.

Kritchevsky, Sybil; E. Prescott; and L. Walling. *Planning Environments for Young Children: Physical Space* (Second edition). Washington, D.C.: National Association for the Education of Young Children, 1977.

Vergeront, Jeanne. *Places and Spaces for Preschool and Primary (Indoors)*. Washington, D.C.: National Association for the Education of Young Children, 1987.

Vergeront, Jeanne. *Places and Spaces for Preschool and Primary (Outdoors)*. Washington, D.C.: National Association for the Education of Young Children, 1988.

CHAPTER 5

Staff Training

Arns, Betsy. *Training School-Age Child Care Teachers*. Huntington Beach, Calif.: School-Age Workshops, 1991.

Jones, Elizabeth. *Teaching Adults: An Active Learning Approach*. Washington, D.C.: National Association for the Education of Young Children, 1986.

Ranson L., and P. Salisbury Hedges. *Program Development for School-Age Children Caregiver Book and Trainer's Guide*. Stillwater: Child Care Careers, Inc., Oklahoma State University, 1989.

Assessment and Evaluation

"Appropriate Assessment Practices for Young Children." Program Advisory, FSB 92/93-01. Sacramento: California Department of Education, July, 1992.

Bloom, Benjamin, and George F. Madaus. *Evaluation to Improve Learning*. New York: McGraw-Hill, 1981.

Legal Advisory on Assessment. LO: 2–92. Sacramento: California Department of Education, November 30, 1992.

McLaughlin, Milbery W., and David C. Phillips. *Evaluation and Education: At Quarter Century*. Chicago: University of Chicago Press, 1991.

"Retention of Students in Elementary and Middle Grades." Program Advisory, CIL: 91/92-02. Sacramento: California Department of Education, September 16, 1991.

Sisson, Linda. *Kids Club: A School-Age Program Guide for Directors*. Nashville: School Age Notes, 1991.

CHAPTER 6

Parent Involvement

California Strategic Plan for Parental Involvement in Education. Sacramento: California Department of Education, 1992.

Frede, Ellen. *Getting Involved: Workshops for Parents*. Ypsilanti, Mich.: High/Scope Press, 1984.

Handbook on Parent Education. Edited by Marvin J. Fine. San Diego: Academic Press, Inc., 1980.

Honig, Alice S. *Parent Involvement in Early Childhood Education* (Revised edition). Washington, D.C.: National Association for the Education of Young Children, 1979.

Parent Involvement Programs in California Public Schools: Families, Schools, and Communities Working Together. Sacramento: California Department of Education, 1991.

Parents Are Teachers, Too. Sacramento: California Department of Education, 1984 (brochure). Available also in Cambodian, Chinese, Hmong, Japanese, Korean, Laotian, Pilipino, Portuguese, Spanish, and Vietnamese.

Powell, Douglas R. *Families and Early Childhood Programs*. Washington, D.C.: National Association for the Education of Young Children, 1989.

The Second Handbook on Parent Education: Contemporary Perspectives. Edited by Marvin J. Fine. San Diego: Academic Press, Inc., 1988.

Stone, Jeanette G. *Teacher-Parent Relationships*. Washington, D.C.: National Association for the Education of Young Children, 1987.

U.S. Department of Health and Human Services. *A Parent's Guide to Day Care*. Washington, D.C.: U.S. Government Printing Office, 1980.

Early Adolescent Resources

Ames, Louise B.; Frances Ilg; and Sidney M. Baker. *Your Ten to Fourteen Year Old* (Revised edition). New York: Delacorte Press, 1989.

Caught in the Middle: Educational Reform for Young Adolescents in California Public Schools. Sacramento: California Department of Education, 1987.

Dorman, Gail. *3:00 to 6:00 p.m.: Planning Programs for Young Adolescents* (Revised edition). Carrboro: Center for Early Adolescence, University of North Carolina at Chapel Hill, 1986.

Lefstein, Leah M., and Joan Lipsitz. *Programs for Young Adolescents.* Carrboro: Center for Early Adolescence, University of North Carolina at Chapel Hill, 1986 (catalog).

Musson, Steven, and Maurice Gibbons. *The New Youth Challenge: A Model for Working with Older Children in School-Age Child Care.* Nashville: School Age Notes, 1988.

Multicultural Education

Alike and Different: Exploring Our Humanity with Young Children (Revised edition). Edited by Bonnie Neugebauer. Washington, D.C.: National Association for the Education of Young Children, 1992.

Allen, Judy; Earldene McNeill; and Velma Schmidt. *Cultural Awareness for Young Children* (Revised edition). Dallas: CAYC Learning Tree, 1981.

Derman-Sparks, Louise, and the A.B.C. Task Force. *Anti-Bias Curriculum: Tools for Empowering Young Children.* Washington, D.C.: National Association for the Education of Young Children, 1989.

Discover the World: Helping Children Develop Respect for Themselves, Others, and the Earth. Edited by Susan Hopkins and Jeff Winters. Philadelphia: New Society Pubs., 1990.

Ramsey, Patricia G. *Teaching and Learning in a Diverse World.* New York: Teachers College Press, Teachers College, Columbia University, 1986.

A World of Difference: A Teacher-Training Prejudice Awareness Program to Combat Discrimination and Value Diversity. New York: Anti-Defamation League, 1991 (training materials).

York, Stacey. *Developing Roots and Wings: A Trainer's Guide to Affirming Culture in Early Childhood Programs*. St. Paul, Minn.: Redleaf Press, 1992.

York, Stacey. *Roots and Wings: Affirming Culture in Early Childhood Settings*. St. Paul, Minn.: Redleaf Press, 1991.

Catalogs and Newsletters

After-School Activities (newsletter). School-Age Workshops, P.O. Box 5012, Huntington Beach, CA 92615-5012.

After-School Catalogue, 1401 John Street, Manhattan Beach, CA 90266.

Report on School-Age Child Care (newsletter). Business Publishers, Inc., 951 Pershing Dr., Silver Springs, MD 20910-4464; telephone 1-800-274-0122.

School Age Notes, P.O. Box 40205, Nashville, TN 37204 (newsletter, publications, and other resources).

Program Evaluation or Accreditation Materials

Exemplary Program Standards for Child Development Programs Serving Preschool and School-Age Children (1991)

Available from:

California Department of Education
Bureau of Publications, Sales Unit
P.O. Box 271
Sacramento, CA 95812-0271
(916) 445-1260

Accreditation Criteria and Procedures (Revised edition, 1991)

Available from:

National Academy of Early Childhood Programs
Division of the National Association for the Education of Young Children
1509 16th Street, NW
Washington, DC 20036-1426
(202) 328-2601

ASQ: Assessing School-Age Child Care Quality

Available from:

Wellesley College School-Age Child Care Project, Wellesley College
Wellesley, MA 02181

Developmentally Appropriate Practice in School-Age Child Care Programs (1993)

Quality Criteria for School-Age Child Care Programs (1991)

Available from:

Project Home Safe
American Home Economics Association
1555 King Street
Alexandria, VA 22314

School-Age Care Organizations

California School Age Consortium, 111 New Montgomery Street, Suite 302A, San Francisco, CA 94105 (newsletters, technical assistance, and training).

National School-Age Child Care Alliance. For Membership Department, write c/o California School Age Consortium (see address above). Address all other inquiries to NSACCA, c/o Tracey Ballas, 1942 Norwood Boulevard, Zanesville, OH 43701.

Professional Play Leaders Association USA, P.O. Box 161718, Austin, TX 78716 (newsletter, training, and other resources on leadership in play and adapting activities for developmental needs).

Research and Training Organizations

Center for Early Adolescence, University of North Carolina at Chapel Hill, Carr Mill Mall, Suite 211, Carrboro, NC 27510

University of California, Irvine, School-Age Care Project, Department of Education, University of California, Irvine, Irvine, CA 92717-5500

Wellesley College School-Age Child Care Project, Center for Research on Women, Wellesley College, Wellesley, MA 02181-8259

Videotapes and Games

Exemplary Program Standards: How to Conduct Your Agency Self-Study. Sacramento: California Department of Education, 1991. Videotape.

Porter, Rick. *Roughhousing.* Austin, Tex.: Professional Play Leaders Association USA, 1989. Videotape.

Square One T.V. Super Kit (Math). New York: Children's Television Workshop, 1991. Videotape, Activity Cards, Games.

Therrell, Jim. *The Essentials for Play Leadership.* Austin, Tex.: Professional Play Leaders Association USA, 1989. Videotape.

3-2-1, Contact Action Kit (Science). New York: Children's Television Workshop, 1991. Videotape, Activity Cards.

Publications Available from the Department of Education

This publication is one of over 600 that are available from the California Department of Education. Some of the more recent publications or those most widely used are the following:

Item no.	Title (Date of publication)	Price
1151	Adoption Recommendations of the Curriculum Development and Supplemental Materials Commission, 1994: Follow-up Adoption, Science (1994)	$5.50
0883	The Ages of Infancy: Caring for Young, Mobile, and Older Infants (videocassette and guide) (1990)*	65.00
0973	The American Indian: Yesterday, Today, and Tomorrow (1991)	6.50
1079	Beyond Retention: A Study of Retention Rates, Practices, and Successful Alternatives in California (1993)	4.25
1067	California Private School Directory, 1993-94 (1993)	16.00
1086	California Public Education: A Decade After A Nation at Risk (1993)	4.75
1091	California Public School Directory (1994)	16.00
1017	California State Plan for Child Care and Development Services Funded Under Federal Block Grant (1991)	5.50
1036	California Strategic Plan for Parental Involvement in Education (1992)	5.75
0488	Caught in the Middle: Educational Reform for Young Adolescents in California Public Schools (1987)	6.75
0874	The Changing History–Social Science Curriculum: A Booklet for Parents (1990)	10/5.00†
1053	The Changing History–Social Science Curriculum: A Booklet for Parents (Spanish) (1993)	10/5.00†
0867	The Changing Language Arts Curriculum: A Booklet for Parents (1990)	10/5.00†
1115	The Changing Language Arts Curriculum: A Booklet for Parents (Korean) (1993)	10/5.00†
0928	The Changing Language Arts Curriculum: A Booklet for Parents (Spanish) (1991)	10/5.00†
0777	The Changing Mathematics Curriculum: A Booklet for Parents (1989)	10/5.00†
0891	The Changing Mathematics Curriculum: A Booklet for Parents (Spanish) (1991)	10/5.00†
1142	The Changing Mathematics Curriculum: A Booklet for Parents (Korean) (1994)	10/5.00†
1072	Commodity Administrative Manual (1993)	13.00
0978	Course Models for the History–Social Science Framework, Grade Five—United States History and Geography: Making a New Nation (1991)	8.50
1034	Course Models for the History–Social Science Framework, Grade Six—World History and Geography: Ancient Civilizations (1993)	9.50
1132	Course Models for the History–Social Science Framework, Grade Seven—World History and Geography: Medieval and Early Modern Times (1994)	12.75
1093	Differentiating the Core Curriculum and Instruction to Provide Advanced Learning Opportunities (1994)	6.50
1045	Discoveries of Infancy: Cognitive Development and Learning (videocassette and guide) (1992)*	65.00
1098	English as a Second Language: Implementing Effective Adult Education Programs (1993)	6.00
1046	English-as-a-Second-Language Model Standards for Adult Education Programs (1992)	7.00
0041	English–Language Arts Framework for California Public Schools (1987)	5.00
1056	Essential Connections: Ten Keys to Culturally Sensitive Care (videocassette and guide) (1993)*	65.00
1011	Exemplary Program Standards for Child Development Programs Serving Preschool and School-Age Children (1991)	5.50
1124	Exemplary Program Standards for Child Development Programs Serving Preschool and School-Age Children (Spanish) (1994)	5.50
1010	Exemplary Program Standards: How to Conduct Your Agency Self-Study (1992)	14.95
1106	Exemplary Program Standards: How to Conduct Your Agency Self-Study (Spanish) (1993)	14.95
0751	First Moves: Welcoming a Child to a New Caregiving Setting (videocassette and guide) (1988)*	65.00
0839	Flexible, Fearful, or Feisty: The Different Temperaments of Infants and Toddlers (videocassette and guide) (1990)*	65.00
0804	Foreign Language Framework for California Public Schools (1989)	6.50
1116	The Framework in Focus: Answers to Key Questions About the English–Language Arts Framework (1993)	5.50
0809	Getting in Tune: Creating Nurturing Relationships with Infants and Toddlers (videocassette and guide) (1990)*	65.00
1089	Greatest Hits in Environmental Education (1993)	7.00
1083	Handbook for Teaching Vietnamese-Speaking Students (1994)‡	5.50
1064	Health Framework for California Public Schools, Kindergarten Through Grade Twelve (1994)	8.50
0734	Here They Come: Ready or Not—Report of the School Readiness Task Force (Full Report) (1988)	5.50
0712	History–Social Science Framework for California Public Schools (1988)	7.75
1154	Home Economics Education Career Path Guide and Model Curriculum Standards (1994)	17.00
1114	Implementation of Middle Grade Reforms in California Public Schools (1993)	6.50
1071	Independent Study Operations Manual (1993)	30.00
0878	Infant/Toddler Caregiving: A Guide to Creating Partnerships with Parents (1990)	10.00
0880	Infant/Toddler Caregiving: A Guide to Language Development and Communication (1990)	10.00
0877	Infant/Toddler Caregiving: A Guide to Routines (1990)	10.00

*Videocassette also available in Chinese (Cantonese) and Spanish at the same price.
†The price for 100 booklets is $30; the price for 1,000 booklets is $230. A set of one of each of the parent booklets in English is $3; a set in Spanish is also $3.
‡Also available at the same price for students who speak Cantonese, Japanese, Korean, Pilipino, and Portuguese.

Item no.	Title (Date of publication)	Price
0879	Infant/Toddler Caregiving: A Guide to Setting Up Environments (1990)	$10.00
0876	Infant/Toddler Caregiving: A Guide to Social–Emotional Growth and Socialization (1990)	10.00
1128	Instructional Materials Approved for Legal Compliance (1994)	14.00
1024	It's Elementary! Elementary Grades Task Force Report (1992)	6.50
1147	It's Elementary! (Abridged Version) (1994)	3.50*
0869	It's Not Just Routine: Feeding, Diapering, and Napping Infants and Toddlers (videocassette and guide) (1990)†	65.00
1104	Just Kids: A Practical Guide for Working with Children Prenatally Substance-Exposed	8.25
1107	Literature for History–Social Science, Kindergarten Through Grade Eight (1993)	8.00
1066	Literature for Science and Mathematics (1993)	9.50
1033	Mathematics Framework for California Public Schools, 1992 Edition (1992)	6.75
1113	On Alert! Gang Prevention: School In-service Guidelines (1994)	6.50
1065	Physical Education Framework for California Public Schools, Kindergarten Through Grade Twelve (1994)	6.75
0845	Physical Education Model Curriculum Standards, Grades Nine Through Twelve (1991)	5.50
1119	Prelude to Performance Assessment in the Arts (1994)	8.00
1032	Program Guidelines for Individuals Who Are Severely Orthopedically Impaired (1992)	8.00
1094	Program Quality Review Training Materials for Elementary and Middle Level Schools (1994)	7.50
1048	Read to Me: Recommended Readings for Children Ages Two Through Seven (1992)	5.50
0895	Recommended Readings in Spanish Literature: Kindergarten Through Grade Eight (1991)	4.25
1149	Resource Guide, 1994-95: Conferences, Workshops, and Training Opportunities for District and County Business Office Staff (1994)	5.50
0753	Respectfully Yours: Magda Gerber's Approach to Professional Infant/Toddler Care (videocassette and guide) (1988)†	65.00
1118	Roads to the Future: Final Report (1994)	10.00
1117	Roads to the Future: Summary Report (1994)	8.00
1127	Sampler of History–Social Science Assessment—Elementary, A (Preliminary edition) (1994)	8.25
1125	Sampler of Science Assessment—Elementary, A (Preliminary edition) (1994)	9.00
1088	School District Organization Handbook (1993)	16.00
1042	School Nutrition Facility Planning Guide (1992)	8.00
1038	Science Facilities Design in California Public Schools (1992)	6.25
0870	Science Framework for California Public Schools (1990)	8.00
1040	Second to None: A Vision of the New California High School (1992)	5.75
0980	Simplified Buying Guide: Child and Adult Care Food Program (1992)	8.50
0752	Space to Grow: Creating a Child Care Environment for Infants and Toddlers (videocassette and guide) (1988)†	65.00
1043	Success for Beginning Teachers: The California New Teacher Project, 1988–1992 (1992)	5.50
1134	Teachers' Catalog of Grants, Fellowships, and Awards (1994)	5.50
1044	Together in Care: Meeting the Intimacy Needs of Infants and Toddlers in Groups (videocassette and guide) (1992)†	65.00
0846	Toward a State of Esteem: The Final Report of the California Task Force to Promote Self-esteem and Personal and Social Responsibility (1990)	5.00
0758	Visions for Infant/Toddler Care: Guidelines for Professional Caregiving (1989)	6.50
0805	Visual and Performing Arts Framework for California Public Schools (1989)	7.25
1016	With History–Social Science for All: Access for Every Student (1992)	5.50
0989	Work Permit Handbook (1991)	7.75
1073	Writing Assessment Handbook: High School (1993)	9.25

*Also available in quantities of 100 for $20 (item number 9838); 500 for $80 (item number 9839); and 1,000 for $155 (item number 9840).
†Videocassette also available in Chinese (Cantonese) and Spanish at the same price.

Orders should be directed to:

California Department of Education
Bureau of Publications, Sales Unit
P.O. Box 271
Sacramento, CA 95812-0271

Please include the item number for each title ordered.

Mail orders must be accompanied by a check, a purchase order, or a credit card number, including expiration date (VISA or MasterCard only). Purchase orders without checks are accepted from governmental agencies only. Telephone orders will be accepted toll-free (1-800-995-4099) for credit card purchases only. Sales tax should be added to all orders from California purchasers. Stated prices, which include shipping charges to anywhere in the United States, are subject to change.

Publications Catalog: Educational Resources and its supplement contain illustrated, annotated listings of departmental publications. Free copies may be obtained by writing to the address given above or by calling (916) 445-1260.

92-56 003-0049-94 9-94 5M